FAITH
EXTENDERS

FAITH EXTENDERS

Everyday Ways To Increase Your Faith

By
John Avanzini

HIS Publishing Company
Hurst, Texas

Faith Extenders —
Everyday Ways To Increase Your Faith

ISBN 1-878605-05-4

HIS Publishing Company
P. O. Box 1096
Hurst, Texas 76053

*This book is lovingly dedicated to
Martina Yvette Avanzini,
my loving daughter and faithful secretary
and a woman of strong faith.*

Table of Contents

Table of Contents

Foreword

This is not a book about theories that no one has tried or ideas that don't seem to work right. This is a practical book written by a man who practices what he teaches. I know John Avanzini well—he has been with me on the air many times. I've watched him face difficult challenges and get through them by using his faith to tap the power of God.

That's what *Faith Extenders* is about. As Christians we have no guarantee that our lives will be problem-free—all positives and no negatives. The Bible shows us that even the strongest believers had to go through hard times. But how they magnified faith to overcome obstacles is a lesson many of us have not learned.

John Avanzini has mined from Scripture the secrets of how to act in ways that make our faith grow stronger. Using examples from the lives of Bible heroes, he shows us how to extend our faith by using the power of our imagination. He instructs us in the proper use of word pictures in increasing faith. His stories and examples convince us that we can see our faith grow by taking some simple but important steps.

We are so impressed with the great men and women of the Bible that we easily forget they were flesh-and-blood people just like us. They experienced pain and loss; they were afraid; they worried about their children; they were proud, envious and angry; they failed; they sinned. Then what made them heroes? It was their ability to turn to God and receive His blessings. They had a measure of faith as we do, but they were able to extend it. In *Faith Extenders*, John Avanzini prepares us to live by the same principles, to face whatever comes with strong vibrant faith reaching out to the Lord.

Paul Crouch
Founder and President
Trinity Broadcasting Network

A Personal Word From the Author

The apostle Paul loved books. This is evident from the instructions he gave his young friend and co-laborer Timothy in his last epistle:

> Bring the cloak that I left with Carpus at Troas when you come—and the books, especially the parchments (2 Tim. 4:13, NKJV).

The books, no doubt, were the works of writers who had especially blessed the apostle with their revelation and inspiration. The parchments he spoke of were written copies of the revelations that God had given Paul.

I hope you share this same passion for good books and for God-given revelation. I believe this book will become a treasure to you to strengthen and extend your faith.

I am praying that your faith will become strong enough to reach across the chasm of doubt and circumstances which lies between your need and God's yet unmanifested supply and bring you victory.

> For whatsoever is born of God overcometh the world: and this is the victory that overcometh the world, even our faith (1 John 5:4).

Further, God tells us that, unless we have faith, we cannot please Him.

But without faith it is impossible to please Him: for he that cometh to God must believe that he is, and that he is a rewarder of them that diligently seek him (Heb. 11:6).

With these and other clear biblical declarations of the absolute necessity of faith, it is almost unbelievable that so many Christians continue to be faithless. They hope that somehow they will please God with lives almost void of any real Bible faith. Yet the precious Word of God states that without this wonderful thing called faith it is impossible to please Him.

All through Scripture we are exhorted to develop strong faith—until it matures into the same kind of faith God has.

And Jesus answering saith unto them, Have faith [margin, 'the faith of God'] (Mark 11:22).

We must all be careful to seek the leading of the Holy Spirit as we read God's Word and particularly books about His Word. As we begin this study together, I encourage you to seek the leading of the Holy Spirit and to open your spirit and mind to His direction. Let us never make decisions about the mind of God by the mere wisdom of men.

I am praying that you will harvest rich blessing and "hidden manna" from each page of this book. I am also praying that you will put these principles and concepts to work in your life.

Remember what He said:

According to your faith be it unto you (Matt. 9:29).

In Christian love,

John F. Avanzini

Acknowledgement

*Senior chief Gregory Bucher
and his faithful wife, Barbara, who diligently
helped me to complete this manuscript*

CHAPTER ONE

What Are
Faith Extenders?

Throughout the Scriptures, God has used the most ingenious extenders or amplifiers of our faith. His Word abounds with illustrations of these "little helpers." These helpers magnify our faith, coaxing it upward to a higher level. He does this so we can make the transition from the realm of the natural to the superior realm of the supernatural.

God has spread these wonderful faith intensifiers throughout His Word so that we cannot help but conclude they must be of great importance to us. With these ingenious intensifiers, He desires to help us develop stronger faith. He gives us these helpers—*faith extenders*, if you please—to amplify and stretch our weak faith into strong faith. These faith extenders help us overcome the ever-present hindrances of doubt and unbelief sent from Satan to weaken our faith and separate us from God's best. They amplify our faith so it can combat the constant invasion of fear, doubt and unbelief more effectively.

Faith extenders are not the product of my excited imagination. I have not learned about faith extenders from someone else's book. Nor have I learned about them from other men. They were revealed to me directly from the Scriptures. There is ample evidence God has used them throughout the ages and He means for us to use them today.

They are intended as tools to help the saints develop strong faith.

These truths about faith extenders are not "secret" truths. Nowhere in Scripture are they spoken of as mysterious. They are used openly throughout the entire Word of God. They are on the surface awaiting your discovery.

From Doubting Thomas to Witnessing Thomas

> Then said he to Thomas, Reach hither thy finger, and behold my hands; and reach hither thy hand, and thrust it into my side: and be not faithless, but believing (John 20:27).

A very clear example of our Lord using a faith extender is found in the account of Thomas, when Jesus was dealing with his doubts about His resurrection. Keep in mind that at the time of this discourse, Thomas's faith had become extremely weak. The glaring circumstances that surrounded the crucifixion and burial of Christ had overcome his faith. His faith was so weakened by doubt he could not even begin to believe the account of the resurrection given to him by his most trusted friends—friends who were eyewitnesses to the resurrection.

With Thomas's faith in this critical state, the Lord knew it would soon sink into terminal unbelief. It was at this crucial point He administered a most effective amplifier to Thomas's faltering faith.

The amplifier Jesus used was His own nail-punctured hands and wounded side. Immediately, Thomas's faith was lifted to a point where it could bridge the chasm between the natural and the supernatural. When Thomas imagined his finger entering the cruel puncture wound in the hand of our Lord, his faltering faith exploded into the strongest of faith—faith that easily made the quantum leap from the impossibilities of mortality thinking to the possibilities of immortality thinking. From one moment to the next, Thomas's depleted spiritual batteries came up to full charge.

Please take note. This did not take two or three days; it was instantaneous! That simple faith extender (just twenty-five words) ignited the almost-extinct faith of the apostle Thomas. It had the same effect on his faith that the great booster rockets have on lunar spaceships—quickly pushing them out of earth's gravitational pull to soar in the heavenlies.

The simple faith extender Jesus used on Thomas that day jet-propelled him beyond the unbelief of his doubts into the strongest of faith in our Lord's resurrection. I am convinced that Thomas is in heaven today because he had strong enough faith to overcome doubt and to believe in the actual resurrection of Jesus Christ.

When our Lord asked Thomas to put his finger in the nail holes of His hands, Thomas's weak faith revived. Thomas's faith was instantly amplified and expanded by this faith extender.

How crude it must have seemed to the other disciples when our Lord invited the doubt-dominated Thomas to do this thing. But how welcome it was to Thomas when he could cast off stubborn doubt and take on overcoming faith.

Child of God, just keep in mind that Jesus wasn't nearly as interested in proper etiquette as He was in reviving Thomas's fainting faith. Our Lord knew when Thomas's faith was strengthened it would lift him out of the darkness of doubt into the marvelous light of resurrection life—a life that can only be entered into by strong faith.

Some of the faith extenders we study will have a more personal impact on you than others. They will become even more exciting as you learn how to adapt them to your own circumstances. These faith extenders will allow you to

3

reach out with new determination for the good things of God. Like Thomas of old, the use of simple faith extenders will boost your faith.

God is no respecter of persons (Acts 10:34).

Faith extenders will turn your weak faith into strong faith. Their possibilities are almost limitless. With faith extenders, you have the potential of developing faith that overcomes the world!

How Faith Extenders Work

Faith extenders operate in much the same manner as a modern sound system. Modern sound systems are made up primarily of a microphone, amplifier and speaker. When a person speaks through the microphone of a sound system, his normal voice level is amplified or expanded far beyond its normal volume. When the sound emerges, it becomes many hundreds of times louder than when it was originally spoken.

Another example of how faith extenders work is seen in the operation of an electric transformer. A transformer's purpose is to bring back to full power electric voltage which has suffered a voltage drop. The electric transformer has the ability to multiply and intensify electrical current which is passed through it, thereby bringing it back to full power and offsetting the drop in voltage caused by resistance. This resistance occurs as the current flows from one point to another along transmission cables. In that same way, faith extenders intensify or bring again to full power our faith—faith which can become weakened by the resisting circumstances that confront us.

This book will help you observe the overwhelming evidence from Scripture that attests to the legitimacy of faith extenders. After reading this book and applying its principles, there will be no room left for doubt as to their validity. You will be convinced of their value in helping you build the strong faith you desire. You will see the benefits of faith extenders to yourself and to other Christians. The benefits will be obvious as they help change your imperfect faith from glory to glory in a reflection of His perfect faith.

Bread-Breaking Breaks Blindness

Jesus was the master at using faith extenders. He never seemed to be without them. Whenever a need arose, He produced them quickly and effortlessly.

For example, Luke 24:13-35 tells us of a time after Jesus' resurrection when He was walking with two of His disciples on their way to Emmaus. Their faith was so weak at this time that they were unable to believe in His reported resurrection. These same disciples had seen Him raise the dead, feed the 5,000 and work other miracles. At this time, however, their faith couldn't rise above the glaring circumstances of the crucifixion and burial of Jesus. Their faith had degenerated to nothing more than a whimsical wish.

We trusted [note past tense] that it had been he which should have redeemed Israel (Luke 24:21).

They had no faith to believe in the redemption which their Lord had before purchased for them.

This encounter on the Emmaus Road must have been a very depressing one. How amazing! Three years of personal teaching and demonstration of His power had seemingly come to nothing. What had gone wrong? Had Jesus failed? Why were these handpicked leaders at such a low point? How had they come so short of the strong faith needed to sustain them at this most important time? How would these faithless, confused men be able to evangelize a hostile world—a wicked world that had just a few days before, in the cruelest manner, snuffed out all their hope on a crude Roman cross?

Let me make this very clear: Jesus had not failed! Neither had these men failed. What had failed was their faith. Their once strong faith had been greatly weakened by the harsh circumstances surrounding the death of Jesus. Their faith was now at the point of being extinguished.

Notice the resiliency of faith and how quickly it responds to proper stimulation. Amazing as it may seem, it was revitalized with nothing more than a fleeting glance of a very simple faith extender.

Let me explain as we join them in their journey. Notice how our Lord points to the weakness of their faith:

> O fools, and slow of heart to believe (Luke 24:25).

Then He expounds to them His fulfillment of all things.

> And beginning at Moses and all the prophets, he expounded unto them in all the scriptures the things concerning himself (Luke 25:27).

After all this teaching by the greatest teacher, Jesus, their faith still shows no sign of regaining its potency. The teaching session continues until evening. As they reach their lodging, they invite Jesus (whom, amazingly, they still do not recognize) to stay the evening with them.

This invitation is extended to Him strictly out of courtesy, not because they recognized Him. Isn't this amazing? The best teaching by the best teacher was totally ineffective at strengthening their faith.

But now observe how quickly this subliminal faith extender He uses catapults their faith to new heights:

> And it came to pass, as he sat at meat with them, he took bread, and blessed it, and brake, and gave to them. *And their eyes were opened* and they knew

6

him; and he vanished out of their sight (Luke 24:30-31, italics mine).

When Jesus broke the bread, their eyes were opened! Amazing as it may seem, once again Jesus made faith extenders out of His nail-pierced hands.

Take your hands and hold them as if you were breaking a small loaf of bread. Notice that before the bread is broken, the backs of your hands are primarily visible to yourself. However, as you begin the rotating motion of your hands to break the loaf of bread, the rotation causes the backs of your hands to be shown to everyone around you.

As Jesus broke the bread, the backs of His hands became the focal point. They became clearly visible to everyone at the table—hands with ugly, gaping holes in the backs of them—holes that were made by the harsh Roman spikes. Think of how ragged those puncture wounds must have been. The holes would have been exceptionally harsh where the cruel spikes exited His hands before entering the cross. With the sight of those gaping holes in the backs of his hands, a giant burst of spiritual adrenaline surged through their weak, faltering faith.

Like high octane gasoline on a failing fire, spontaneously their flickering faith exploded once again into a roaring blaze. There they were openly displayed before them— the nail-scarred hands of their Lord. With this done, the Scriptures say, He was gone. He vanished! He could now go because the much-needed work was done. Their once-weak faith was now back to full power. The canyon of doubt and unbelief had been bridged by a single glance at the backs of His nail-pierced hands.

Before you become skeptical, read carefully the following Scripture portion:

And they said one to another, Did not our heart *burn*

within us, while he talked with us by the way, and while he opened to us the scriptures? And they rose up the same hour, and returned to Jerusalem, and found the eleven gathered together, and them that were with them, saying, the Lord is risen indeed, and hath appeared to Simon. And they told what things were done in the way, and how He was known of them in breaking of bread [literally, 'when He broke the bread'] (Luke 24:32-35).

Now, with their heads held high and a new determination in their step, they were on their way to Jerusalem to begin the era of the greater works. Now they, who could only refer to His resurrection as a wish, were clearly and boldly declaring as irrefutable the fact that Jesus was risen from the dead.

The renewed faith of these disciples testifies to the effectiveness of faith extenders. Now please note that this is not an assumption on my part. The showing of His nail-scarred hands was most definitely the thing that regenerated their faith—"he was known to us in the breaking of bread."

Faith Extenders Are Needed by All

Realistically speaking, I know of no one with such consistent faith that he or she could not regularly use some good faith amplifiers. As you read, allow yourself to gain new insights into faith extenders. Allow them to help you develop a more effective level of faith.

The apostles, when they requested that the Lord increase their faith, were aware of the constant necessity for their faith to be increased.

And the apostles said unto the Lord, Increase our faith (Luke 17:5).

Simon Peter said that we can have the same kind of faith

the apostles had.

> Simon Peter, a servant and an apostle of Jesus
> Christ, to them that have obtained like precious faith
> with us through the righteousness of God our Savior
> Jesus Christ (2 Pet. 1:1).

In the Gospel of Mark, the father whose son had a demonic spirit said, with tears in his eyes, "Lord, I believe; help thou mine unbelief" (Mark 9:24).

Wise Christians should quickly learn that faith extenders are a very important part of their spiritual arsenal. Faith extenders can help them maintain strong faith so they can more effectively wage the good fight of faith against all the enemies of their souls. Faith extenders are needed by all saints.

CHAPTER TWO

Substitution,
Verbalization and Imagination

Without doubt, God is the greatest teacher who has ever been or ever will be. And Jesus is the full manifestation of all the teaching attributes of God. No one will ever compare to Him as our favorite teacher.

I am sure, however, that you have some other teacher from whom you especially enjoy learning. Undoubtedly, this person is adept at using various object lessons to impress upon minds the points he is making.

For example, if your favorite teacher would say, "The track star was running very fast," he would probably position his body as if they were actually running and would probably make some of the gestures a runner makes. If, on the other hand, he wanted to impress his students with the fact that something he was describing was very hot to the touch, he might reach out, pretending to touch an imaginary object and would then shake his hand violently in a gesture of pain. His action would amplify your comprehension of the hot object. These are amplifiers. They might be verbal and/or visual. They are common intensifiers that all good teachers use to increase their students' comprehension.

I repeat, God is the greatest of all teachers. He uses these same kinds of intensifiers. And He also uses object substitutions to assist floundering faith. These object substitutions help us to grasp hold of the things that await us just beyond the natural realm—in the supernatural realm. He also uses verbalization (speaking) of the yet unmanifested as if it were already done.

Many uninformed saints, as well as unbelieving scoffers, openly ridicule believers for speaking in the present tense of those things that are yet future. However, God actually encourages this type of speaking (the verbalization of the yet unmanifested).

Let me demonstrate with a hypothetical illustration. God might say to you, "You have a great ministry." Your natural mind immediately will say to you, "I don't have a ministry." But, notice, with the speaking of these words, God has planted a seed-thought of a ministry in your mind, right into your imagination. With this new stimulation, you now begin to look for a ministry—not just any ministry, but your ministry. Notice the progression. Not only has the seed-thought of your ministry been planted, but anticipation of your ministry has been activated. With the speaking of that which does not yet exist, God has planted the seed that will one day be your ministry. Granted, this seed may be weak, but, nevertheless, as you water this verbal seed with your anticipation, it germinates. As you look and believe for your special ministry, to your amazement and the amazement of others, it will appear.

When God makes this kind of statement, He puts a very powerful and complex procedure into motion. This new ministry won't start in the natural realm, but it will begin quietly in the spiritual realm.

Let's look more closely at this process.

As God speaks His yet unmanifested plan for your life, His revelation sparks anticipation inside of you—anticipation that is actually a part of faith. While the next statement is my own, I emphasize that it is very important to grasp its significance. *The presence of anticipation immediately calls the thing anticipated to be manifest.* The pre-declaration of God's intention to bring forth your ministry develops and strengthens your faith's potential for receiving.

I hope you can see that the positive declaration that your ministry now exists is a much-needed step forward—a step that moves you from simply desiring a ministry to having a ministry. Granted, it is a small step, a first of many steps that must be made before your ministry is fully manifested. The first step is probably not even measurable by human technology. But always remember that when you deal with faith, it takes a very small measure of faith to activate great power. For faith of just a mustard seed size can move the largest of mountains all the way to the sea.

> And Jesus said unto them...if ye have faith as a grain of mustard seed, ye shall say unto this mountain, remove hence to yonder place; and it shall remove; and nothing shall be impossible unto you (Matt. 17:20).

Child of God, be assured this is not some off-the-wall illustration. It demonstrates one of the unique characteristics of God's nature which is to speak things that by all outward appearances are nonexistent as though they already existed. The conception of everything He has ever brought into existence has always been His spoken word.

That God speaks those things that are not yet as though they already existed can be documented from Scripture. For example, God plainly referred to Gideon as "thou mighty man of valour":

> And the angel of the Lord appeared unto him, and said unto him, the Lord is with thee, thou mighty man of valour (Judg. 6:12).

Now it just so happened Gideon was a coward at the

time God spoke of him as a "mighty man of valour."

Hear the words of the apostle Paul as he explains that God does this:

> God, who quickeneth the dead, and *calleth those things which be not as though they were* (Rom. 4:17, italics mine).

See how this tremendous power of God can ignite your imagination with visions of God's will for your life. Now add to this the drawing power of anticipation which will result from those visions. I am speaking of a biblically founded process that God uses daily. This faith-expanding procedure (faith extender) will quickly take you out of the bush leagues of weak faith into the world series of strong faith. Let your imagination portray God's promises for you. Let these vivid mind-pictures ignite your anticipation of them.

Anticipation is one of the chief ingredients of what the Bible calls faith.

> Now faith is the substance of things hoped for [that which you actively anticipate], the evidence of things not seen (Heb. 11:1).

Right in your Bible are the primary components of faith—anticipation (things hoped for). Whenever your anticipation level is heightened, your faith level is heightened.

While we are at this point, let us also notice that faith's other component is the evidence of the unseen. Your imagination supplies you with a mental picture (evidence) of the thing God promises to supply.

Notice that there are some who would surrender the use of this most holy process to the occult because they have counterfeited it. These false teachers have called it positive thinking, cybernetics or whatever name they might give their counterfeit. I will not answer those who would give up our right to this process. I will let the Bible speak to this matter.

> Behold, I come quickly: hold that fast which thou hast (Rev. 3:11).

I hope this admonition doesn't fall on deaf ears, for our precious Lord was the one who said it.

Remember God's Word on pre-declaration of the as yet unmanifested.

> Surely the Lord God will do nothing, but he revealeth his secret unto his servants the prophets (Amos 3:7).

With this firmly in mind, our prayer should be:
"Dear Lord, speak freely to me the yet unmanifested things and I will repeat them boldly, for I do want to fulfill Your word in Ephesians to imitate You."

> Be ye therefore followers [imitators] of God, as dear children (Eph. 5:1).

Mind Pictures

Everyone has an imagination. When it is used properly, it can transcend the invisible realm of the mind and enter the visible realm of the physical world. Let me illustrate.

It is a very natural thing that, prior to learning to drive an automobile, young people become engrossed in imagining and anticipating the day they will actually be involved in the hands-on experience of driving a car. It is amusing to watch teenagers or preteens as they, with single-minded concentration, imagine the big day they will actually be driving. I have noticed that when their concentration becomes strong enough, they will play-act their desires. All of a sudden, they will bring the noises from their silent, invisible imagination into the visible realm. You hear them "vrrroom! vrrroom!, honk! honk!" These sounds are almost always coupled with the full animation of gear shifting, hand signals and steering wheel maneuvers. Their imagination is set aflame by their immense anticipation. The mind pictures become so vivid that they cannot keep from playacting the whole process of driving a car.

The casual observer may not catch the total significance of this phenomenon when they see it in action. You see, imaginations are invisible. They live in the mind. But, as they are stimulated by strong anticipation, a strange phenomenon occurs. The non-substantive imagination jumps from the invisible, intangible realm of the mind into the tangible, visible realm of the conscious world.

Suddenly the invisible gear shift is at the fingertip of the prospective driver. Imaginary traffic becomes so vivid that the invisible steering wheel, which is being tightly held, must be operated to avert collision after collision. The roar of the engine bursts forth into the air and resounds on the ears of those who are in the room.

Do you see the transformation taking place? I might say that when this process reaches this advanced stage, it won't be long before it is manifested. Now, granted, it is not as yet complete. But anyone will have to admit that this potential driver has set a much more effective course toward being an early driver than the person who never thinks of driving or anticipates the day they will drive. This is not to say that the person who never uses his imagination will never drive. But it shows that:

For as he thinketh in his heart, so is he (Prov. 23:7).

Misused Imagination

If this process wasn't powerful and valid, God wouldn't warn us not to misuse our imagination. God commands us to cast down certain imaginations because of the vast power our imagination, coupled with anticipation, has to draw that which we imagine and anticipate into our everyday experience.

> Casting down imaginations, and every high thing that exalteth itself against the knowledge of God, and bringing into captivity every thought to the obedience of Christ (2 Cor. 10:5).

Any thinking person who reads the above verse can surely see that the power of imagination is great. God wants us to keep that part of our mind which has the ability to visualize things that do not yet exist clear of all images contrary to God's will. God is especially concerned that our imaginations be kept clear of images of the things the devil or the flesh desires to manifest in our lives. God's desire for our imaginations is an uninterrupted picture of the beautiful things in our lives. This is one of the ways God uses the natural operation of our minds in conjunction with the supernatural operation of His mind to bring us into His perfect will. This joint venture of His mind and our mind works to strengthen our faith. Following this process will keep us on course and on schedule with the good life which God has planned for each of His children. Just listen to the quality of life God wants for His children.

> I am come that they might have life, and that they might have it more abundantly (John 10:10).

> According as his divine power hath given unto us all things that pertain unto life and godliness, through the knowledge of Him [His mind in us] that hath called us to glory and virtue (2 Pet. 1:3).

The world has a saying, "An idle mind (imagination) is the devil's workshop." While this is a secular saying and not found in the Bible, it is, nevertheless, a true saying.

That is why God speaks the following through the apostle Paul:

> Finally, brethren, whatsoever things are true, whatsoever things are honest, whatsoever things are just, whatsoever things are pure, whatsoever things are lovely, whatsoever things are of good report; if there be any virtue, and if there be any praise, think on these things (Phil. 4:8).

Just picture how great life would be for you and for all the saints of God if we could always think on *true* things, *honest* things, *just* things, *pure* things, *lovely* things of a *good report*, and *virtuous* things. All these are attributes of God and worthy of *praise*. If this took place, it wouldn't be long until the very kingdom of God would manifest itself. Clearly, the apostle Paul has good reason for admonishing us to keep our imagination and thought processes cleared of every thought or imagination that would dare to contest the knowledge of God.

The apostle John emphasizes the benefit of the inner man being occupied with godliness in the following verse:

> Beloved, I wish above all things that thou mayest prosper and be in health, even as thy soul prospereth (3 John 2).

You see, prosperity and health depend on your soul prospering. Now hear with anointed ears the words of Paul:

> Casting down imaginations, and [even] every high thing that exalteth itself against the knowledge of God, and bringing into captivity every thought to the obedience of Christ (2 Cor. 10:5).

What wonderful instructions Paul gives pertaining to the disciplining of our imagination apparatus. In 2 Corinthians 10:4, he speaks of the weapons of our warfare not being carnal, but mighty to the "pulling down of strongholds" (those things that take strong holds upon our thought processes).

Then, in verse five he continues with "casting down imaginations." These are not just any imaginations, but the particular imaginations that exalt themselves against the knowledge of God, literally *the knowledge of God that you individually possess*. God wants to cast down every thought that forms an obstacle between you and His will. Give attention to His final instruction, "bringing into captivity every thought (every single thought) to the obedience (attentively making every thought harken to and obey the instruction) of Christ."

God wants to use your powerful thought processes (imagination and anticipation) to strengthen your faith. If you will allow Him to do this, then He can, through your strong faith, manifest all the good things He has for you.

I hope you can better understand why God wants you to use the powerful faith extender of your anticipation-stimulated imagination to keep your faith at full strength.

One Step Deeper

Grasping the following statements will allow you to understand the greatness of your imagination and the part it plays in the building of your faith.

We hear from God's Word that faith is the substance (the basic raw material) of which *everything is made*. We also learn from Scripture the two very important dimensions of any object which exists in the universe:

Number one—*substance*.
Number two—*evidence* of existence.

A picture of something is considered to be good evidence that it exists. Everything that now exists in visible form

19

(the whole universe) has at least these two dimensions—substance and evidence. Hebrews 11:1 tells us that everything exists or existed in the invisible realm before it appears in the visible realm.

Note that invisible things are becoming visible every day. Actually, this process is accelerating. Many never-before-existent things are coming into existence every moment. For instance, every building that has ever existed or now exists, in the whole world, always exists in the invisible world of the imagination of the builder or architect long before it exists in the visible realm. Every process, every product, every invention, every organization, everything that is added to the earth by mankind exists in the invisible realm of the imagination of man before it can enter the visible, tangible realm.

Allow your spirit to take hold of that truth. Allow natural information to stimulate revelatory knowledge.

What sensory mechanism (our ability to sense things) operates as a laboratory for this activity? I propose to you that it is your imagination. Your imagination is the picture tube that receives and disseminates all the many actions of revelation, memory and reason which form the mental pictures of that which you desire. These pictures, if agitated by anticipation, then stimulate a series of thoughts and actions which will bring the invisible will of God into manifestation.

When this process is complete, the thing pictured in your imagination, which is seen only by you, will be seen by others. Notice that your imagination operates absolutely in parallel and harmony with your faith. For "faith is the *substance* of things hoped for, the *evidence* of things not seen." Imagination gives *substance* to the things that you desire (hope for). It provides the *evidence* of things not seen (those things that are either as yet nonexistent or, as yet, not in your possession).

I submit to you that your imagination is a very special, highly spiritual apparatus. It is an apparatus whose purpose is the enhancing of your faith and the aiding of the process of bringing the invisible things into the visible realm.

To prove this, allow me to use a strange illustration. The reason I must do this is that, as yet, nothing exists which comes even close to illustrating the operation of man's imagination. The example I am about to use did come from the imagination of man; therefore, maybe it will be effective.

In the science fiction television series "Star Trek," the spaceship Enterprise was equipped with many mind-boggling pieces of equipment: special force shields, anti-matter motors, and the like. Nothing on that ship, however, was as powerful a part of its operation as the imaginary apparatus they called the "transporter." This apparatus supposedly was able to transport people and things from one part of the universe to the other. It was supposed to de-materialize a person or object in one place and re-materialize them in another. Supplies could be transported from one place to another. People could be moved rapidly from a place of danger to safety. All of this was accomplished by the use of the "transporter."

Now let's leave the realm of science fiction and return to the realm of reality and see how this illustration might help to clarify what I am saying to you about your imagination. Your imagination is nothing more than a *transporter*. This God-given apparatus, when operated properly and in accordance with God's instructions, can bring the invisible good things of God one step closer to the realm of the visible. With that said, I must, however, also remind you that it can, when operated wrongly, bring the evil things of the flesh from the invisible realm one step closer to the visible realm.

The Courthouse of Imagination

See this process at work in Scripture. Jesus said that to look on the opposite sex with lust is to commit adultery with them "in your heart" (imagination).

But I say unto you, that whosoever looketh on a woman to lust after her hath committed adultery with her already in his heart (Matt. 5:28).

Note this statement very carefully. Not every case of adultery manifests itself in the visible realm. But every case of adultery that takes place manifests itself in the invisible realm (imagination). Also, every case of adultery that takes place in the visible realm first took place in the invisible realm (in the imagination of the guilty person or parties).

Notice that an act in the imagination is evidence enough to convict of great sin. Let's allow our Lord to take this principle further. To hate a brother is to murder him. The Word of God says visions of hatred bring indictment in the court of God.

Whosoever hateth his brother is a murderer (1 John 3:15).

Every thought of hatred of a brother or sister results in murder in the invisible realm. But not every act of murder takes place in the visible realm.

Child of God, remember that God holds a permanent viewing permit to every showing of your imagination. Remember that He is the discerner of the thoughts and intents of our hearts.

It is of eternal importance that you understand the full power of your imagination. Your imagination goes beyond the inside of your head. It transcends the natural realm and ascends into the spirit realm. It operates a continual showing of your desires in the very presence of God. Remember this:

The Lord knoweth the thoughts of man (Ps. 94:11).

God intends for us to use our imagination continually to project to our inner man the very will of God for our lives. This is why the Old Testament writer of Proverbs tells us, "Where there is no vision, the people perish" (Prov. 29:18).

The visions of our imagination are extensions of what we desire or what God desires. The desires of the one whose visions are played the most will come to pass in our lives.

Imagination and Time Travel

With a simple operation of our imagination, we can go across the corridor of time and space. We can call Moses and the parting of the Red Sea into our view. Without even a moment's separation, alongside of Moses we can place Samson pulling down the building on the head of his captors. Beside these two, we can place Daniel, safe in a hungry den of lions. Without imagination, we can call all of these events from their resting place in the past to the present. I might note that any or all of those victorious events can, at will, be called up and used as faith extenders.

Proper mental pictures can amplify our faith. These scenes of victory can amplify our faith to part our own Red Sea, pull down the roof on our enemies and give lock-jaw to our lions. What a great producer of faith your imagination can be! Keep a good picture in your imagination of yourself overcoming every foe in the name of Jesus.

FAITH EXTENDERS

Jesus Used Visualization

> And the seventy returned again with joy, saying,
> Lord, even the devils are subject unto us through
> thy name. And he said unto them, I beheld Satan
> as lightning fall from heaven (Luke 10:17-18).

In this discourse, Jesus is speaking more than just
prophetically. Prophecy is the prediction of that which will
happen before it happens. What Jesus speaks here is not
prophecy. Here He is speaking of a yet-to-happen event
which had not yet come to pass as if it had already happened. I am convinced that in Luke 10:18 He was not
prophesying. If Jesus had been prophesying, He would no
doubt have said, "You will soon see Satan fall." Instead,
He places the verb "behold" in its past tense. He says,
"I *beheld* Satan fall." However, the chronological facts
are that almost 2,000 years after Jesus spoke these words
the event He described as being past still awaits its accomplishment in time. For not until the twelfth chapter
of the book of Revelation does this happen.

> And the great dragon was cast out, that old serpent,
> called the Devil, and Satan, which deceiveth the
> whole world: he was cast out into the earth, and
> his angels were cast out with him (Rev. 12:9).

Let's take a closer look at this event. For within it there
lies the revelation of another of the faith extenders that
Jesus used.

> And the seventy returned again with joy, saying,
> Lord, even the devils are subject unto us through
> thy name (Luke 10:17).

The context vividly shows the exuberance of the disciples
upon their return from a most successful ministry campaign. Hear them as they come running to Jesus saying,

24

"Lord, You won't believe what's going on out there. The success of our meetings is beyond our wildest dreams!"

Can't you just hear Jesus as He asks them, "Tell Me, what is happening out there?"

They probably all speak at once, "Lord, we just speak Your name, and things happen! Why, Lord, incurable people are immediately healed, cripples rise up and walk, and desperate people find hope. More amazing than any of this, we simply use Your name and snarling, foaming devils are rendered harmless. Why, in Your name we cast them out of the people effortlessly!"

Now pay close attention and see a faith extender at work in the imagination of our Lord and Savior, Jesus Christ. Notice carefully verse eighteen. He states, without hesitation, that which He has had at the forefront of His imagination ever since the rebellion of Satan and his angels. Now the full impact of this situation doesn't come to us unless we realize that Satan was at that moment still in the heavenlies. Even at this writing, Satan has not yet been thrown out. He is still called the prince of the powers of the air.

Why, then, did Jesus speak of this yet future event as if it had already happened? I think it was to teach us the importance of our imagination in the operation of our faith. Keep in mind that faith is the evidence of things *hoped for*. Jesus lived daily with the anticipation of the fall of Satan and his eventually being cast into the lake of fire.

The Lord kept every thought captive to the obedience of God.

> Casting down [evil] imaginations, and every high thing that exalteth itself against the knowledge of God [notice, this is not knowledge about, but *of* God], and bringing into captivity every thought to the obedience of Christ (2 Cor. 10:5).

Keep in mind that the Lord Jesus was the pattern Son who followed God's instructions exactly. We must also follow Jesus' example and take every stray thought captive.

The divine knowledge spoken of in 2 Corinthians 10:5 is beyond that knowledge attained through human investigation and reasoning. It is the knowledge that God freely gives us through spiritual revelation and inspiration. This divine knowledge will be ours as long as we allow the image-maker within us, our imagination, to be free and clear of anti-God knowledge. With a God-dominated imagination, we can easily bring every thought into submission to Christ. This is in its simplest form nothing more than letting the mind of Christ be in us.

> Let this mind be in you, which was also in Christ Jesus (Phil. 2:5).

Possessing the mind of Christ is critical to operating in the God-kind of knowledge. Be very careful that you do not try to move into the God-kind of knowledge by use of natural reasoning.

> Now we have received, not the spirit of the world [human reasoning and logic], but the spirit which is of God; that we might know the things that are freely given to us of God. Which things also we speak, not in the words which man's wisdom teacheth, but which the Holy Ghost teacheth; comparing spiritual things with spiritual (1 Cor. 2:12-13).

Carefully notice what these verses say: We "know the things that are freely given to us....*Which things also we speak*." When Jesus saw that the disciples had enough faith to speak His name with authority, immediately the Father freely gave Him a vision of Satan falling from heaven—*which thing He also spoke*!

The report from His disciples that they were actually using the name of Jesus in authority over the evil spirit world signified to our Lord that the end of the reign of Satan was now irrevocably set in the earth. This victorious report prompted Jesus to speak that which He had been given freely—a mental picture of Satan falling as lightning from heaven. Remember, up to that very moment the defeat of Satan was only living in the divine mind of God. But with the testimony of the disciples, that in "the name of Jesus" demon forces had to obey them, the doom of Satan was sealed.

At this writing, all saints eagerly await the full manifestation of our Lord's declaration, of seeing Satan fall as lightning from heaven. But notice that the informed saints will go one step further than merely wishing this to come to pass. They will join with Jesus in the use of this great faith extender and boldly speak of Satan's falling from heaven not as a future event but as a past event.

Say it out loud: "Satan, I choose to see you as lightning falling from heaven. I proudly declare that I see you falling out of my heavenlies. God says you will fall. If God says you will, and Jesus says He already has seen you fall, I choose to see you fall. Also, I will not see you powerful. I will see you fallen."

Fix that thought in your imagination. Immediately you feel your inner man leap within you. You can actually feel those positive statements lift your faith to a higher level.

CHAPTER THREE

God Freely Gives Us All Things

Before we can appreciate fully the value of faith extenders, we must understand that our God wants us to have all sufficiency in all things. At this moment in Christ we have no want or need. Hear the Word of God on this matter:

> According as his divine power hath given [past tense, it exists now] unto us all things that pertain unto life and godliness, through the knowledge of him that hath called us to glory and virtue (2 Pet. 1:3).

Notice here that Peter tells us we have all things that pertain to life (natural life) and godliness (spiritual life). This verse, as well as others, speaks of God's desire for us not only to have life, but to supply us with the good life more abundantly. Of course, all of this is predicated on our having the strong faith necessary to receive it. Read Hebrews, chapter 11. It tells of a people who had the abundant supply of God. This was written so we could see that God met their needs and wants. It goes beyond this and says that while it was good for them, God has something even better for us. Let's face it—the good life is for us.

And these all, having obtained a good report

through faith, received not the promise: God having provided some better thing for us, that they without us should not be made perfect (Heb. 11:39,40).

God's Invisible Warehouses

Those who are sincerely striving to reach the mark of the high calling of God in Christ Jesus can be assured that "all things that pertain unto life and godliness" have been given freely to us by our God. These supplies have been set aside for us in the heavenly warehouses of God. They are patiently awaiting our appropriation through strong faith.

God has all the supply you could ever need or want already set aside for you! There is an abundant supply awaiting you. Now hear this: He has an answer for your situation that is bigger than your need and supercedes your want. This source of supply will last you until Jesus returns. All this awaits you at the point in which your faith in God's Word becomes strong enough to swallow up all the doubts of your circumstances.

I can just hear the false reasoning of skeptics saying, "Brother John, 2 Peter 3:1 is speaking in the past tense. This verse means we have already received all things that pertain to life. We will just have to make do with that scant amount until we die or the Lord comes again."

How slowly the traditions of men die. This kind of reasoning can only be put to rest by the cooperation of two things: the opening of your mind and the introduction of Scriptures.

These warehouses exist right now, just outside of the temporary, visible realm in the eternal, invisible realm.

Blessed be the God and Father of our Lord Jesus

Christ, who hath blessed us with all spiritual blessings in heavenly places in Christ (Eph. 1:3).

The apostle Paul says we have all spiritual blessings in
heavenly places. Now this was just another verse to me
until I heard evangelist/teacher Jerry Savelle explain it.
He said that when the Bible refers to all our blessings as
spiritual, this does not mean they are only blessings pertaining to the spirit world. When Paul spoke of all spiritual
blessings, he was not referring to the nature of the blessing. He was speaking of their *state* or *position*. They are
in the state of the spiritual. They are invisible, if you
please. All that is spiritual is at this time invisible.

All these many blessings are laid up for us in heavenly
places in the spirit world. They are safely being cared for
in God's warehouses in the heavenly realm. These warehouses are full to the brim with everything we will ever
need or want. All of our yet unacquired blessings are there
in inventory, awaiting requisition by our strong faith. It
is God's responsibility, as Father, to provide them, but
it is our responsibility, as sons, to bring them forth from
their invisible state in the heavenlies. We, as sons, must
bring them into the natural, material world where we can
put them to work and enjoy their benefits.

In his discourse on faith, Savelle went on to explain that
the process of bringing these invisible blessings into the
visible state was only accomplished by faith.

Now faith is the substance of things hoped for, the
evidence of things not seen (Heb. 11:1).

He points out that faith is the substance, the raw material,
of things hoped for and the evidence of things not seen.
The things not seen are those things which comprise our
yet unfulfilled desires. It is strange, with all the light being shed on the fact of God's abundant supply, that the
children of God hang on stubbornly to the kind of thinking

which binds them to chronic insufficiency. What is even more amazing to me is the fact that they boast of their unscriptural walk in insufficiency as "suffering for Jesus." This must grieve our Lord who has already gone through the insufficiency for us.

> For ye know the grace of our Lord Jesus Christ, that, though he was rich, yet for your sakes he became poor, that ye through his poverty might be rich (2 Cor. 8:9).

Are your present circumstances what God intended them to be? Do you possess all things that you need for life and godliness? Aren't there a number of things in both these realms that you need? Hear the Word of God as it speaks again of God's willingness to supply your desires.

> For all things are yours, whether Paul, or Apollos, or Cephas, or the world, or life, or death, or things present or things to come; all are yours (1 Cor. 3:21,22).

God's Word boldly says all things are yours—past, present and future. Not one of your needs or wants should go unprovided.

But remember what we have been learning. All of this supply comes to us by strong faith. Let me encourage you: this truth is becoming more evident by the day. Everywhere I go it is evident that the saints are learning to reach, with ever-increasing faith, into God's great, invisible warehouses. They are, by faith, materializing more and more of the much needed supply which has so long eluded the church. That which was only hoped for a generation ago is now being manifested. Remember: "Faith is the substance [raw material, as Savelle says] of things hoped for, the evidence of things not seen [of their existence in the invisible realm]."

As the church goes from glory to glory, the Lord deals with the saints with more and more maturity. God, who is a Spirit, now deals with us on an increasingly higher spiritual level. In times past, He condescended to mankind's natural level when communicating with them. This is what He did when He sent His Word—Jesus—to become flesh. He now, however, wants to end the condescending. For the last 2,000 years He has been calling us up to His faith level, to learn a new existence in the heavenlies with Him. His preference is not to come down to the level of our old circumstance-dominated natures. Instead, He wants us to come up to his circumstance-dominating nature. He wants our needs to be supplied by the superior methods of the spirit realm.

We are being called upward—from glory to glory into His marvelous image (2 Cor. 3:18). He is not interested in doing those things that promote what you were, instead He is calling you up to that which you are destined to be. He now insists on supplying your wants and needs by a spiritual process.

> Blessed by the God and Father of our Lord Jesus Christ, who hath blessed us with all spiritual blessings in heavenly places in Christ (Eph. 1:3).

Quality Supply Awaits

By now, you should be getting it into your spirit that your God is ready, willing and able to supply you with everything you need and want. Let's now go a step further into the realm of God's supply. Not only does God want to supply your needs and wants, but He wants to supply them with the best of supplies.

> But my God shall supply all your need according to His riches in glory by Christ Jesus (Phil. 4:19).

33

Notice carefully that God does not say He will supply your needs out of His riches in glory. He says He will supply your needs *in accordance with* His riches in glory. God is speaking of supplying your needs and wants in abundance. Here He is not addressing the quantity of His supply, but He is speaking of the quality of that supply. What the apostle Paul is telling us in this verse is plain. Your God-provided portion will be of the highest quality. It will be of the same quality as His riches are in glory.

Tradition teaches that God supplies our needs out of His riches in glory. This would be impossible because of two things: first, it would necessitate a decrease of God's possessions. This would be an impossibility; He never decreases in anything. A daily diminishing of God's net worth is not possible. Second, the word "according" is used. By definition, this speaks of quality not quantity. Clearly, Paul is speaking of the high quality of our supply and not the mere quantity of our supply.

Lay a strong hold upon the next statement I will make for it is very significant. God does not decide the quantity of your supply! Hold onto your hat. Don't allow traditional concepts to make the Word of no effect. You decide the quantity of your supply. The measure of your giving decides the measure (quantity) of your receiving.

> For with the same measure that you use, it will be measured back to you (Luke 6:38, NKJV).

Just let that thought sink in. We will get back to it later.

If you are ready for another shock, let's move on. The traditional interpretations of Philippians 4:19 must be removed for it to become effective to each of us. Tradition teaches that the verse promises to *all* saints that God shall provide all their needs. This is a wrong interpretation of this verse. It is not the apostle's intention to convey any such thought to the body of Christ. What Paul is saying here is clear when the fourth chapter is read in its full context. The context of this verse begins in Philippians 4:15:

> Now ye Philippians know also, that in the beginning of the gospel, when I departed from Macedonia, no church communicated with me concerning giving and receiving, but ye only. For even in Thessalonica ye sent once and again unto my necessity. Not because I desire a gift: but I desire fruit that may abound to your account. But I have all, and abound: I am full, having received of Epaphroditus the things which were sent from you, an odor of a sweet smell, a sacrifice acceptable, well-pleasing to God. But my God shall supply all your [the mission givers] need according to his riches in glory by Christ Jesus (Phil. 4:15-19).

With the whole context in mind, we can clearly see who qualifies as the beneficiaries of Philippians 4:19. The passage in Philippians 4 teaches that this promise is for those who faithfully helped by supporting Paul in his world outreach of Christian missions. Notice, he says that the Philippian saints were the only ones who gave to his missionary journey which began in Macedonia. Also, it might be noted that it was not just a one-time gift which qualified them for these quality blessings, for once and again they ministered to his need. Paul here speaks specifically to the Philippian saints. The application of this verse *applies to all saints who qualify* by regularly giving to world evangelism.

So, with this said, let me summarize Philippians 4:19. It clearly speaks of a quality of supply (the best of the good life) to those who seriously and consistently give to those ministries which go into the regions beyond, preaching Christ to the yet unsaved.

Surprised? You shouldn't be. Everyone knows God's things (His riches in glory) are good things. Like every good father, He desires to supply His obedient children (those who regularly give to world evangelism) with quality things—things that are in kind with His glorious possessions. He takes no morbid pleasure in seeing His child struggling with poor quality goods, run down at the heels, run off at the sides and looking like a mile of bombed-out runway.

Here is what I am saying in a nutshell: God not only wants you to have all things, but, glory to God, He wants you to have the best of all things.

We know that God's things are good things. If God drove up right now in His chariot (if He drives a chariot), I guarantee you that all the spokes would be in the wheels. He surely does not ride around with missing spokes, a bent fender, slick tires and a bumper sticker that reads, "Well, Praise God Anyhow." Read about it throughout Scripture. God lives a very high quality life-style. His is a quality existence, filled with abundance—literally, "more than enough" of the very best.

Unless you have strong faith, you will not be able to give abundantly and liberally to evangelizing the world. Without strong faith, it is impossible to tithe to your local church, much less give generously and regularly to other ministries.

It is easy to say that God supplies our needs. However, it is difficult to believe (strong faith) that God supplies all our needs. It will take the strongest of faith to bring forth as a reality in your life the promise of God to "supply all your needs in accordance with His riches in glory."

The faith that brings forth the life-style described in Philippians 4:19 will be strong enough to overthrow every negative circumstance which challenges the validity of God's Word.

I do hope that all of this is enlightening you as to the value of faith extenders. I hope you are already seeing some ways in which they can be used to amplify your faith. Let your own faith extenders prepare your faith for the rewarding spiritual work of manifesting the superabundant blessing that God has for you.

> Now unto him that is able to do exceeding abundantly above all that we ask or think, according to the power that worketh in us [our faith] (Eph. 3:20).

CHAPTER FOUR

Faith Extenders
Used by Abraham

The use of faith extenders to strengthen our personal faith is found from one end of the Scriptures to the other. Throughout the Old Testament, prominent Bible characters time and again used faith extenders. Let us observe Abraham, the father of our faith, and see how he used faith extenders to magnify and multiply his faith.

Stars and Sand as Faith Extenders

When God gave Abraham the covenant promise of a son being born to him and his wife, Sarah, He also gave him two powerful faith extenders to keep that promise ever strong within Abraham. Our heavenly Father knew that Abraham would need the strongest of faith in order to keep on believing God's promise throughout the years that lay between the promise of the son and his birth. If Abraham, *the father of our faith*, was given faith extenders to keep his faith strong, then we, as his heirs, must realize the important part they play in building and maintaining strong faith.

The two faith extenders that Abraham received from God were the stars of the heavens and the sands of the seashore.

That in blessing I will bless thee, and in multiplying

I will multiply thy seed as the stars of the heaven, and as the sand which is upon the sea shore; and thy seed shall possess the gate of his enemies (Gen. 22:17).

At first observation, it would seem that God had given two faith extenders to Abraham that pertained to the same thing, the birth of his son Isaac. But, upon closer observance, we can understand that they spoke of two entirely different things. They represented the fact that there would be two kinds of seed brought forth. One would be a natural seed—like the earth, earthy (sand of the seashore). The other would be like the heavens, heavenly (the stars of the sky). Now, notice, these faith extenders were not given because of Abraham's two heirs, Ishmael and Isaac.

Let's compare spiritual things to spiritual.

Not in the words which man's wisdom teacheth, but which the Holy Ghost teacheth; comparing spiritual things with spiritual (1 Cor. 2:13).

I would like to propose that one of Abraham's two "natural born" sons (Ishmael) was not involved in the faith extenders of the stars and the sand. These two faith extenders were given to Abraham as part of an *everlasting covenant*. They were not given as a covenant that would only extend to the birth and posterity of his two sons. I want you to know that these two faith extenders were given to show Abraham continuously that there would be two Israels—his natural-born heirs, who were to be multiplied as the sands of the seashore, and his spiritual-born heirs, who were to be multiplied like the stars of the heavens.

Ishmael was conceived of Sarah's handmaiden, Hagar. His birth came about by a lack of faith and not by any means strong faith. These two faith extenders were given to Abraham so he would know that his son would come without fail, and with him would come two powerful forces—one natural, one spiritual—one a nation called Israel, the other a nation called the church.

> And if ye be Christ's, then are ye Abraham's seed,
> and heirs according to the promise (Gal. 3:29).

Let the Scripture expand upon this point. When we compare spiritual things with spiritual things, we realize that the sand of the earth has always symbolized the natural man.

> And the Lord God formed man of the dust of the
> ground (Gen. 2:7).

> The first man is of the earth, earthy...As is the
> earthy, such are they also that are earthy (1 Cor.
> 15:47,48).

Without question, the sands of earth symbolized Abraham's natural descendants.

Just as surely, the stars of the heavens, or heavenlies, are symbolic of the spiritual man (the saints of God).

> And those who are wise—the people of God—shall
> shine as brightly as the sun's brilliance, and those
> who turn many to righteousness will glitter like stars
> forever (Dan. 12:3, TLB).

The people who turn many to righteousness are those who are righteous, the saints of God.

Just think of it: God, in His lovingkindness, gave Abraham not only two faith extenders, but He gave him two *constant* faith extenders—the stars by night and vast sandy landscape by day. No matter where Abraham sojourned or what he was doing, these two constant faith extenders witnessed to him each day of his life.

Can't you just see him traveling through the desert day after day looking at the sand and meditating on the promise of God. His thoughts were constantly occupied with the necessity of his becoming a father.

Then, each night, as the stars shone, a faith extender of glorious splendor would fill the sky. How much these two faith extenders must have comforted and encouraged Sarah and Abraham, as over and over again they witnessed God's marvelous promise to them—the promise that their seed would bring forth two great nations, Israel and the church.

Praise God, that we, as the body of Christ, are the stars of the promise. We are Abraham's seed.

> If ye be Christ's, then are ye Abraham's seed, and heirs according to the promise (Gal. 3:29).

Abraham and Lot

Faith extenders played a significant part in developing and preserving Abraham's strong faith. Notice in Hebrews 11 how Abraham's faith stayed stronger than Lot's through the use of faith extenders.

> By faith he sojourned in the land of promise, as in a strange country [notice that he never allowed himself to become attached to the local population], dwelling in tabernacles with Isaac and Jacob [notice that he kept his son and grandson out of the systems of that land], the heirs with him of the same promise: For he looked for a city which hath foundations, whose builder and maker is God (Heb. 11:9,10).

The Bible clearly teaches that Lot did not separate himself and his family from the world system. Both Abraham and Lot came out from among the heathen in Ur of the Chaldees. But observe the great difference. Abraham remained separated from the heathen. The Bible says that Abraham dwelt in a tent, as a stranger to the land's inhabitants. Lot, however, allowed himself to become re-involved with the heathen. He dwelt in one of the heathen cities and co-mingled his life and family with the heathen population.

The choice that Lot made was his own. Lot, however, had not been given the land; but he was allowed to stay wherever he wished, for Abraham gave him first choice as to where he wanted to live. Remember, it was Lot's free choice when he looked down at the plains of Sodom and Gomorrah and chose to live in and among the inhabitants of those two wicked cities. He could have chosen anywhere, but he decided to become a *fellow citizen* with the heathen. Lot's choice changed his relationship with the land. The choice he made was much different from that of Abrahams. Lot's association with the land became temporary, while Abraham's became eternal.

> While we look not at the things which are seen, but at the things which are not seen: for the things which are seen are temporal; but the things which are not seen are eternal (2 Cor. 4:18).

Abraham stayed out of the world system, giving him an advantage over Lot.

Abraham used another great faith extender. This faith extender kept him from making the same mistake Lot made. Observe carefully as we identify the second faith extender: he "looked for a city whose maker is God" (Heb. 11:10). Notice the Bible says, "*is* God" and not "*was* God." Also, observe that the city which Abraham focused on only had foundations; it was not completely visible. Therefore, he chose to live in a tent. While living in this tent, he was continually awaiting (hoping for) the manifestation of the city that God was building. Lot chose a city which was complete and very visible. Lot's choice necessitated no faith at all.

For we are saved by hope; but hope that is seen is not hope: for what a man seeth, why doth he yet hope for? (Rom. 8:24).

Let's go back to our text in Hebrews 11:10, which says that Abraham "looked for" a city which had foundations (a just-begun city that would only be concluded in these last days), whose builder and maker is God. Abraham had in his mind's eye (his imagination, if you please) a picture of God's city (the new Jerusalem). Because of this mental picture, he would not allow himself to live in a finished house or in a finished city. Instead, Abraham chose to live in a tent outside the gates of the cities of that land. He rejected the distractions of the world's cities. Instead, he eagerly awaited, with anticipation, the coming city of God. His tent reminded him that his permanent dwelling place was yet to come. His faith remained strong by the reminder of his tent, a faith extender, and his anticipation, another faith extender, as he awaited the day he would live in the city of God.

The vision of God building a city was to him a mentally pictured (imagined) faith extender. The daily reality of dwelling in a temporary tent kept him desiring to inhabit a house in a city, not just any city, but the city of God. Had he inhabited that temporal city of the heathen, it would have caused him to lose the vision of God's coming, eternal city.

Abraham extended his faith into the future. He kept his faith in God's promise of a city strong and fresh. Through strong faith, he was able to refuse the *temptation of the present* world.

Contrary to this, Lot surrounded himself with the Sodomites and eventually could not stand in God's promise of a coming city. Because his faith was weakened by heathen influences, his house perished.

Just as God used visions with Abraham, God would have us use visions to extend our faith—nothing elaborate, just simple things to remind us of His will. Just think how valuable the as-yet-unfinished city of God, in which Abraham lives, had become.

New Names Extend Faith

Anyone who is even vaguely familiar with the Bible will know the names of Abraham and Sarah. But how many know that at one time they were named Abram and Sarai? This great faith extender goes unnoticed to all but the most careful students of the Word. God used the changing of their names as great faith extenders. The name Sarah means "little princess." Now keep in mind that, at the time of this name change, she was anything but a little princess. She was actually about ninety years old. Abraham's name change happened when he was about ninety-one years old. His new name, Abraham, means "father of many nations." The full account of this changing of names is recorded in Genesis 17:5,15.

One day, God made a very special visit to His servant, Abram, and his wife, Sarai. At the conclusion of that most significant visit, God said (and I paraphrase), "Old man and old woman, you are most surely going to have that child I have been promising you all these years." By now, this often repeated prophecy was so far past the time of possibility that the Scripture says they both just laughed.

They said (in so many words), "Lord, please be serious about this thing. We cannot have a child. Can't you see that? We are much too old. Why, we're both many years past the age of childbearing."

With this mentality, they never would be able to have a child. Their confession was destroying their faith in God's promise. If the prophecy was to become a reality, they would have to start speaking as if they were going to have a child.

Can't you just see them in your mind's eye (imagination)? There was old Sarai—well past her years of bearing children, her dimming eyes looking across the yet childless room at poor, old, worn-out Abram. Now watch the effect as God interjects a pair of powerful faith extenders. He says to Sarai, "From now on, Abram will call you *princess*" (the literal meaning of her new name, Sarah), "and you, Sarah, will call him *father of many nations*, or Abraham." Can't you just imagine the scene as it unfolds in the dwelling place of that ancient couple? Hear God as He coaxes them to use the new names He has just given them: "Come on now; let's hear you refer to each other by your new names."

Hear Abraham as he reluctantly says, "Hi, Sarah!" (now remember what he was actually saying in the Chaldean language was "Hi, princess!"). Before you can grasp the full impact of this new name God has given to Sarai, you must bring to mind what a princess really is. She is the young daughter of a king—a daughter who is just at the bloom of her youth. She is fully capable of propagating the lineage of the king with the birth of an heir. What a giant contradiction this new name was to the overwhelming circumstances which so long had challenged the faith of old Abram and his ancient wife, Sarai. Keep in mind that every day their increasing age spoke loudly to them of the impossibility of the promise of God. Remember, the promise was that this old woman and this old man would have a son who would be the beginning of a nation of millions and millions of people.

Hear Sarah as she reluctantly tries Abram's new name, "Oh, father of many nations!"—(Abraham in the Chaldean language). Notice the unspeakable wisdom of God. These new names became a constant challenge to the contrary effects of their advanced age. With each use, these highly descriptive new names refuted the negative confession which had become so commonplace with Abraham and Sarah. Remember, before these new names were introduced, their faith was at its lowest point. Their circumstances had tainted their own opinion of the promise of God. They were both laughing openly at the aspect of God's promise ever being fulfilled.

Slowly, but surely, as they used these new names, their attitudes changed. The possibility of the promises of God being fulfilled once again flourished with the use of these new names. Imagine with me, if you would, the amazement of the servants and the neighbors in and around Abraham's encampment. See the scene as Abraham is in the field. Sarah calls out to him, "Oh, father of many nations!" (Abraham). You have to know that a tremendous impact was registered in his mind as this very prolific description of him stirred his imagination. Not only was his imagination stirred up, but the imagination of everyone within earshot of Sarah's calls was affected. Soon, at the sound of his new name, he would straighten up his physical posture to that of a much younger man. Surely, he would pull in his stomach and move with a bit more spring in his step.

As time passed, they kept on referring to each other in that same way, calling back and forth to each other with these highly descriptive new names, until one day, as Abraham passed Sarah's tent, he looked in the curtain and his heart leaped as he realized something had changed. No doubt, his attitude had changed about himself, and now, to his surprise, his attitude was changing about her; and her attitude was changing about both of them. With all this verbal attention to her desirability, no doubt, she started dolling up a bit. I am sure that she now acted a bit more like a princess than an old woman. Can't you just hear him as he gasps and says, "My, Sarah, you really are a princess. Why, you're beginning to look more like a princess every day''? Abraham's desire for her stirred within him until there was aroused that which seemingly had been lost with age.

Can't you just hear the conversation between Abraham and Sarah's contemporaries? "There they go again. Just listen to our leader's wife. I think she's losing her grip on reality. But have you noticed she's not the only one? Just listen to him when he answers with those comments about her being his little princess.''

Why, it probably wasn't long until rumors were flying about the camp that their old chief and his old wife still seemed to have an active sex life. The rumors became so expanded that anticipation of Sarah's having a child bloomed throughout the camp. Hebrews 11:1 began to operate. Faith (the substance of things hoped for) was working all around this great couple. Abraham began to think of himself as "the father of many nations," and Sarah once again pictured the son that God had promised as a possibility.

These images of their virility gave new strength to the overcoming faith of this man of God. Now this spiritual principle is not new to Scripture. For the Scripture bears it out in two places.

> For as he [a person] thinketh in his heart, so is he (Prov. 23:7).

> For verily I say unto you, That whosoever shall say unto this mountain, Be thou removed, and be thou cast into the sea; and shall not doubt in his heart, but shall believe that those things which he saith shall come to pass; he shall have whatsoever he saith (Mark 11:23).

These two verses describe a phenomenon which is now,

in this last part of the twentieth century, being used internationally by secular motivators. While they use it, they don't give credit to the writers of Proverbs or Mark as being the first to have penned this great thought. You see, these truths are so powerful and universal in their application that they are becoming axioms in sociology and human behavior. Even science and medicine can prove that what you say governs what you are and what you are becoming. They also know that what you think greatly affects what you are.

Death and life are in the power of the tongue (Prov. 18:21).

Life and death most certainly were in the tongue of Abraham and Sarah. Life was in the words of faith (the "life" of a great nation, yet unborn). Just as "death" was in their words of doubt, coupled with their laughing at the promise of God.

Remember, you shall have whatsoever you say (Mark 11:23).

Some people might call that lying—calling those things that are not as if they were—but God surely doesn't call it lying, for He is notorious for calling those things that are not as though they were. He boldly and consistently declares the existence of things before they exist.

Even God...calleth those things which be not as though they were (Rom. 4:17).

Now there is no doubt that God had several reasons for changing Abraham's and Sarah's names. I do not mean to say, or even imply, that creating a faith extender was the only reason God had for changing their names. But this name change no doubt had a very positive effect on their faith level. Please note that if God didn't intend for this name change to strengthen their anticipation of His promise, He could have waited until after Isaac was born and then changed their names.

Isaac Sacrificed

> By faith Abraham, when he was tried, offered up Isaac: and he that had received the promises offered up his only begotten son (Heb. 11:17).

This verse states clearly that Abraham offered up Isaac. It does not say he was willing to offer him. It states twice in this same verse that he *actually* offered him up.

The Bible has a great number of good things to say about Abraham. But notice that all of the good things are predicated on the fact that he offered his son Isaac as a sacrifice. This very solemn act of Abraham is the foundation stone for his most favorable relationship with God. God's smile of approval came to him in the act of sacrificing his son Isaac. Now let me re-emphasize that the Bible never indicates that Isaac died. The account says that as Abraham raised the knife to make the fatal plunge into Isaac's heart (Gen. 22:10), the angel of the Lord spoke to him and said, "Don't put that knife into the boy! There is a ram caught in the thicket that will take his place in the sacrifice." Take time later to read the account of Abraham slaying the ram in place of Isaac (Gen. 22:11-13).

The Scripture does not say that Abraham found favor and approval with God when he killed a ram. But it says it was the offering of his son Isaac that won for him the favor of God. The Bible states, without inference to the ram, that Abraham sacrificed Isaac. Now let me ask you how, when and where did he sacrifice his son Isaac?

> By faith Abraham, when he was tried [tested], offered up Isaac: and he that had received the promises offered up his only begotten son (Heb. 11:17).

Isaac was sacrificed "by faith." For we know that faith is the substance of things hoped for and the *evidence of things not seen*. The above verse is the key to the answer of our question. Read it again carefully. It says that by faith Abraham, when he was tried, offered up Isaac; and he that received the promise offered up his only son. The way Abraham offered up Isaac was "by faith." The place that Abraham offered up Isaac was in his imagination—in his heart of hearts. The slaying of the boy was witnessed only by himself and God. You see, it is Jesus who knows the intents of the heart:

> For the word of God is quick, and powerful, and sharper than any two-edged sword, piercing even to the dividing asunder of soul and spirit, and of the joints and marrow, and is a discerner of the thoughts and intents of the heart. Neither is there any creature that is not manifest in his sight: but all things are naked and opened unto the eyes of him with whom we have to do. Seeing then that we have a great high priest, that is passed into the heavens, Jesus the Son of God, let us hold fast our profession (Heb. 4:12-14).

The time of the offering up of Isaac was a prolonged period of time. It began with God first mentioning it to Abraham. For God told him that he would have to offer his son (Gen. 22:2). There was a considerable period of time before they arrived on the mountain and saw the ram. It ends with the voice of the angel of the Lord pointing him to the substitute ram caught in the thicket. Notice in Hebrews 11:17 that this event (the slaying of Isaac) did take place: "when he was tried," he "offered up" Isaac.

In his imagination, time and again, Abraham vividly saw the knife in his son Isaac. Each time, God was the silent witness. The mental picture of his slain son and the envisioning of the brutal wound which the sacrificial knife had made were burned into Abraham's imagination. The picture of this scene of death was so vivid that God received that which was in His servant Abraham's imagination as an actual reality. The human imagination is an apparatus of which we know almost nothing.

God saw what was in the mind (imagination) of Abraham and He saw his determination (his purpose). What He saw was so vivid, so developed and so complete that God received it as an offering of Isaac. Now, notice that the offering of Isaac took great faith. However, it did not just take the blind faith of obedience. But it took Abraham's faith being centered on the fact that God had made promises to him that could only be fulfilled if Isaac lived. Abraham's faith in his son becoming like the stars and sand made him know that God would have to resurrect him from the dead, if necessary, to fulfill the promise of a mighty nation coming forth from his loins.

Notice how very powerful this thing called imagination is. Not one drop of Isaac's blood ever found its way to an earthly altar. Nevertheless, in the imagination of Abraham, where God was ever present, Isaac's blood ran red. Genesis 17:19 states that God would have an everlasting covenant with Isaac and his seed. This could not have been accomplished if Isaac was dead. Abraham's faith was so strong in the promise of God that even if Isaac were sacrificed, God would have had to raise him up again.

However, the sacrifice that was stopped in the natural, visible realm was recorded as done by God, for it had taken place in the imagination of Abraham. Do not assume that the cancelling of this event in the visible realm rendered it cancelled in the invisible realm. Remember, the visible realm is not the primary realm of existence. The visible realm is a secondary realm. It is nothing more than a partial extension of a far greater realm, known as the invisible realm. Strange as it may seem, the visible realm is the Johnny-come-lately of the several realms of existence. The invisible realm is superior in size, age and dimension; for it is eternal.

Proper Words Extend Youth

The process, found in Mark 11:23, of receiving whatsoever you say has worked very satisfactorily in my relationship with my wife, Pat. At this writing, she is approaching her fiftieth year, and she remains delightfully youthful. The preservation of her youth is not just a genetic blessing which she has inherited from her ancestors. For her unmistakable youthful look, even into middle age, is not nearly as noticeable in her ancestors.

For thirty-two years of marriage, I have referred to my wife as "my bride." I have never referred to her as my old lady, the old woman, the war department or any of the other age-inducing names that so many men ignorantly, to their own hurt, call their wives. Each day I have spoken to her with all sincerity of her beauty, her youthful look and her boundless energy. Well, here she is approaching fifty years of age, the mother of five and the grandmother of nine, and she still looks young and beautiful to me and to all who meet her! Many people ask me privately, "Is she much younger than you?"

I have given this personal illustration for two reasons— first to illustrate a point to you, and, second, to reinforce in writing (as a written faith extender) to my lovely wife her youth, health, vitality and my undying love.

A Personal Testimony

Let me close this chapter by sharing with you a very personal time in my own life. What I am about to share will illustrate how a verbal faith extender strengthened my own once-weakened faith.

In my early ministry, my wife, Pat, and I went to a Midwestern city to take the pulpit of a very small church. There were only nine adults meeting in the basement of a rented parsonage. To keep this testimony from taking too much time, I will skip many of the details. It suffices to say that the church grew by leaps and bounds. In just a few years there were well over 1,000 in attendance. We had grown from the basement of the parsonage to the state's second largest auditorium and Sunday school facility. It was a beautiful facility that had been miraculously built with almost all volunteer labor.

However, along with this rapid attendance growth came an even more rapid debt growth. The great adventure became a nightmare. Trouble compounded in every area until the problems that faced us brought us past the limits my faith could bear. In defeat, I resigned that great pulpit. That same year I went back into the business world. I closed the book of my ministry, feeling that I would never again preach the gospel. As far as I was concerned, my best days were now behind me.

Please don't misunderstand—I still loved God. However, with my weakened faith, I could not imagine myself ever again being in the ministry. Every hope was gone. As much as I hate to admit it, I had resigned in disgrace. The great church God had allowed me to build was now in bankruptcy. The wonderful congregation I loved so much was now scattered, leaving many people without a shepherd. My own finances were beyond bankruptcy (to this day, I account our aversion of bankruptcy as one of the formidable miracles of my life). With the best now behind me, I resigned myself to the business world. Now my once divinely appointed life had been reduced to a nine-to-five grind at the corporate treadmill. I am not exaggerating when I say all hope was gone. I couldn't even muster up the vaguest of imagination that God would ever use me again, not even for the simplest of tasks.

In the midst of all this despair, God gave me a verbal faith extender. God gave my good wife, Pat, a vision of us once again in the full-time ministry. In her God-given vision of our new ministry, she vividly saw it greater than anything we had ever done before. With confidence, she spoke of her vision to me. Every day she would say, without emphasis, just quietly, "Our ministry will be bigger than it's ever been." When she would say this I would actually laugh out loud and say to her, "Dream on, dreamer."

I am not exaggerating when I say to you that those few faith-filled words were the only food that my faith received for two and a half years. During that two and a half years, I didn't attend church or fellowship with any of the saints. But each day, Pat would hold back the darkness of unbelief with those powerful words, "John, our ministry will be bigger than it's ever been."

While my natural mind rejected every word of that statement, each word caused my spirit man to leap back from the abyss of total rejection. Each time she made that statement my faith was extended beyond the reach of the ever-present circumstances that were determined to extinguish it forever. Thank God for Pat's wonderful words—wonderful faith extenders—faith extenders that for two and a half years kept my faith alive.

While this verbal faith extender kept my faith alive, God's further plan for our lives was incubating. This time, we would be used in a way that was exactly as the words of her great faith extender had described: "Our ministry will be bigger than it's ever been." Today we are ministering to millions of people, four times each day by television. Our program is seen in almost a thousand communities, as well as in many foreign countries. We speak each week in local churches across America and around the world. Thank God for verbal faith extenders that at strategic times revive faltering faith!

Speaking out loud what God has given as a vision saved my ministry. I hope it can bless you in the hour of your need.

CHAPTER FIVE

Faith Extenders Used in the Wilderness Journey

I am sure, as the Israelites left Egyptian captivity for the promised land, their faith was at its highest level. Their great God, Jehovah, had delivered them out of 400 years of captivity. Not only did He set them free miraculously, but each one of them left Egypt wealthy.

However, as they moved farther and farther from Egypt, their faith diminished. Periodically, they took their eyes off the cloud that went before them. When they did this, they saw the overwhelming circumstances surrounding them. While on this forty-year journey, God repeatedly refreshed their faith with faith extenders. These faith extenders were used to insure that, when they finished their journey, they would finish it in victory. As we examine the faith extenders in this chapter, apply them to your own journey in life. Allow them to raise your faith to a level that no matter what obstacles the enemy may throw in your way, you will be victorious.

The Tabernacle in the Wilderness—a Faith Extender

Exodus chapters 25 through 27 give a detailed description of the tabernacle in the wilderness. It is one of the most elaborate faith-building projects ever used by God. It was a tent-like structure that pictures many truths. It typified the temple of God in heaven, the deity of Christ, the atonement of Christ, the judgment of God, the heavenlies, the substitutionary death of Jesus Christ, the righteousness of the saints, witnessing, salvation, the baptism of the Holy Spirit, the path of the manifested sons into the holy of holies and the body of the born-again believers which forms the temple of God today.

The tabernacle was a model of things which already existed in heaven. The work of the priests, in and around the tabernacle, was typical of the work that our high priest (Jesus) would one day perform for us in the heavenlies. Remember that when Moses was being instructed on how to build the tabernacle, God warned him to follow exactly the pattern of the heavenly tabernacle as shown to him on Mount Sinai.

> ...the example and shadow of heavenly things, as Moses was admonished of God when he was about to make the tabernacle: for, See, saith he, that thou make all things according to the pattern shewed to thee in the mount (Heb. 8:5).

The invisible, heavenly tabernacle was brought into the realm of the visible (the tabernacle in the wilderness) for the purpose of extending and amplifying Israel's faith with a visible manifestation of God's coming salvation. You see, this salvation, which was yet 1,600 years in the future, was at that time totally invisible. Before the tabernacle was described to Moses, it existed only in the mind of God. Because of this, God gave Israel a bigger-than-life faith extender.

There is no way to calculate how effective it was. Every morning when the children of Israel awoke, the tabernacle performed its function as a faith extender. God had ingeniously positioned the tents of Israel so that each day, as they walked out of their tents, the first structure they would see was the tabernacle of God. With every viewing of the tabernacle, the truth of their pending salvation was indelibly impressed upon their imaginations.

Each morning, just like clockwork, they would see the linen cloth stretched around the courtyard of the tabernacle, which testified to the righteousness of the saints. Repeatedly, they would see the bronze sockets, which were a type of the judgment of God. They would see the silver-topped pillars, which were a type of the atonement of God. The herd of sacrificial lambs, outside the entrance to the courtyard, witnessed to them as a type of the sacrificial lamb of God that would some day come. All of these faith extenders kept high their anticipation that the lamb slain from the foundation of the world would one day come and make the eternal atonement that would set the whole world free from sin.

A Continual Aroma Was a Faith Extender

God told the Israelites to make an offering of sacrificial lambs every day. The continual smell of the burning sacrifices made a great faith extender. A lamb was to be burnt "continually" during the day and a lamb was to be burnt "continually" during the night.

And thou shalt say unto them [Israelites], This is the offering made by fire which ye shall offer unto the Lord; two lambs of the first year without spot day by day, for a continual burnt offering. The one lamb shalt thou offer in the morning, and the other lamb shalt thou offer at even;...It is a continual burnt offering, which was ordained in mount Sinai for a sweet savour, a sacrifice made by fire unto the Lord (Num. 28:3,4,6).

We know from God's Word that this sacrifice by fire

was a sweet-smelling savor to God. But don't you also know that the Israelites could smell it. In the vastness of the wilderness desert, the sweet aroma was discernable throughout the encampment. Think of how many times this aroma must have extended their faith and ever witnessed to them that God was protecting them. When a child would awaken in fear during the night, his mother would no doubt comfort him by reminding him of the smell of the roasting lamb, which meant he was under the protection of the God of Israel.

According to Scripture, the leaders, Moses, Aaron and his sons, were the closest to the altar of burnt offerings. To them, the aroma was the strongest. Can't you just imagine the many times they would worry about how to care for such a vast amount of people? As these worries would be discussed among them, no doubt someone would say, "Do you smell the burnt offering? If God plans to sacrifice His son for us, no doubt He cares enough for us to see us through our present circumstances."

Each time the Israelites doubted the only true and living God, they could smell the aroma and be reassured of His love for them. When they were tempted to sin, the aroma was an ever-present help in overcoming temptation. When they did sin, it was an ever-present agent of conviction.

God in His mercy had not only given the Israelites the promises, but, with the promises, He kept their faith strong with a great faith extender. While the nations around them had only gods of wood and stone, they had a living God who communicated with them both actively and passively. He spoke to them actively with His written Word. He also spoke to them passively, with the great faith extender of the tabernacle in the wilderness. These faith extenders daily lifted this fledgling nation above and beyond their everyday circumstances.

Each day, they witnessed the seemingly endless flow of blood upon the altar, the blood of the numerous sacrificial lambs. The lambs' blood only temporarily covered their sins. Day after day, year after year, these object lessons (faith intensifiers) loomed as dynamic reminders from God. In type and in shadow they prepictured the better day that we, the church, now are privileged to live in. Because of this continual reminder, the fledgling nation of Israel was able to stand in faith for 1,600 years, until a woman named Mary had faith to believe the Word of God and conceive in her womb the very seed of God. Jesus is the total manifestation of that to which the tabernacle only eluded.

We cannot deal fully with the myriad faith extenders which are listed in the account of the wilderness journey. It is fertile ground for study.

CHAPTER SIX

Faith Extenders Throughout The Old Testament

The Leader of Millions Needed a Faith Extender

Come now therefore, and I will send thee unto Pharaoh, that thou mayest bring forth my people the children of Israel out of Egypt (Ex. 3:10).

While Moses tended to his father-in-law's sheep on Mount Horeb, God appeared to him and told him that he had been chosen to bring the Israelites out of Egyptian captivity. The story of Moses is a very familiar one. His life took him from a slave's house to a raft in the bulrushes along the Nile to the palace of the king. However, his stay in the palace was not permanent. He would flee the palace, fearing for his life.

As our account of him begins, we find this once-noble prince now tending sheep. No more does he live at the palace of Pharaoh. Now his address is the backside of the desert. From man's viewpoint, he would probably be the poorest possible choice to free God's people and lead them out. Not only is he the poorest choice for a deliverer, but the people he was to deliver were the least likely to follow him. For his own exile was caused by the very people he was now going to attempt to deliver. Consider how low this man's faith level was at the time God told him of the privilege set before him.

> And Moses answered and said, But, behold, they
> will not believe me, nor hearken unto my voice;
> for they will say, The Lord hath not appeared unto
> thee (Ex. 4:1).

God knew that for Moses to become the leader who
would be able to lead the Israelites out of Egyptian captivity, his faith would have to be greatly increased. It would
have to be lifted to supernatural levels far above his confessed unbelief at Mount Horeb. Observe closely as God
gives Moses a faith extender—a faith extender which would
be used time and time again in leading the people of God.

> And the Lord said unto him, What is that in thine
> hand? And he said, A rod. And he said, Cast it on
> the ground...and it became a serpent; and Moses
> fled from before it. And the Lord said unto Moses,
> Put forth thine hand, and take it by the tail. And
> he put forth his hand, and caught it, and it became
> a rod in his hand (Ex. 4:2-4).

I am convinced that every time Moses laid hold of
his shepherd's rod, his mind would immediately rehearse
the miracle of his rod turning into a serpent and his faith
would once again rise into the realm where miracles are
commonplace.

> And thou [Moses] shalt take this rod in thine hand,
> wherewith thou [Moses] shalt do signs (Ex. 4:17).

The Bible records miracle after miracle that Moses performed by extending forth that simple, shepherd's rod. In
Exodus 7:19, the river turned to blood. In Exodus 9:23,
he stretched forth his rod to the sky and thunder, hail and
fire came forth. In Exodus 14:16, he placed his rod in the
Red Sea and millions of Israelites went over to the other

side on dry land, escaping Pharaoh and his thundering army.

Let me show you how to put this Old Testament faith-extending principle to work in your life. Think of past victories God has performed in your life. Maybe your victory is the financial miracle God worked out in the purchase of that new car in the driveway. Don't just look upon it as a car, but let it be a constant witness to you of the fact that God can work the seemingly impossible in your finances. Let it be your special faith extender.

Perhaps your miracle answer to prayer is a beautiful child which the doctors said you would never be able to conceive. Let that child be a constant faith extender. Each time you mention the little cherub's name, let it witness to you of your God's ability to answer prayer.

I am sure that as Moses led the Israelites through the wilderness, there were many times when his faith became weak. But don't you know when it did, he would go over and lay hold of that old shepherd's rod; and as soon as his hands would touch it, his mind would review the past victories in which it had played a part. This rod was a constant visible witness to the presence of his God. For this was not only the rod of Moses but, in the process of turning into a serpent, it had also miraculously become the rod of God. The rod was a continuous witness to the presence of God.

> And Moses said unto Joshua, Choose us out men, and go out, fight with Amalek: tomorrow I will stand on the top of the hill with the rod of God in mine hand (Ex. 17:9).

The next time you feel your faith weakening, go over and pick up the precious cherub God has given you and bring back to your remembrance the miracle that this child is. Never get into that car without thinking that God works financial miracles. See if your faith doesn't immediately rise up within you, strong and renewed. With this strong faith you will be ready to attack, conquer and be victorious over Satan and his tormenting hoard.

Goliath's Head Was a Faith Extender to David

The Old Testament vividly records the account of David defeating the giant, Goliath. It is found in 1 Samuel 17. As we all know, the giant was beheaded at the hands of David, thus ending the days of Goliath's victories. While that day marked the end of the reign of terror by Goliath, it also marked a new day for the conqueror, David. His new life would be filled with fame and multiplied victories over the enemies.

Many wonderful truths come to us from this portion of Scripture. The account of David's encounter with Goliath is well known by the saints. There is, however, some interesting information about this encounter that doesn't lie on the surface. Look with me and see an interesting faith extender.

Notice that for several months following the severing of Goliath's head, David was still carrying the decaying, stinking giant's head with him.

> And David took the head of the Philistine, and brought it to Jerusalem (1 Sam. 17:54).

No doubt, he carried the head in plain view for everyone to see. First, it was a reminder to all who would challenge and oppose him that he routed and killed the dreaded foe, Goliath, and they had better think twice unless the same or worse should befall them. Second, he did not want to forget the power of God that was with him that special day. The giant's head in David's hand was a powerful faith extender. As long as David's hand held the evidence of the decapitation of the champion of the Philistines, the faith of David and the people of God was very high.

It is always in order to keep some mementos of the victories God has given you. They can, time and again, serve you as faith amplifiers. Your personal faith-extending memento might consist of a bill marked "paid"—a bill you thought would never get paid. But, miraculously, God provided the funds to pay it off. That bill, once a Goliath of a debt, can become an aid to your faith. That little piece of paper marked "paid in full" can, time and again, lift your faith to meet every challenge with which the financial realm can confront you.

Maybe your faith-extending memento is a no-longer-needed crutch that you had been told you would always need. But now the dust it collects is a happy reminder of your ability, through faith in God, to appropriate blessings and victory in a time of seeming hopelessness.

Think back often to your special days of victory. We need to recall continuously the victories won by the use of strong faith. Develop a scrapbook which displays your God-given victories. The next time a seemingly insurmountable problem arises, let these mementos remind you of the past victories that strong faith has wrought in your life. Let them extend and amplify your faith to full force so you can confidently face this new challenge. Let the enemies of your faith see the slain Goliaths of your past. But most of all, let yourself see them so your faith can rise to new victories. Place them in conspicuous places— places that your eyes pass over each day.

> And not only so, but we glory in tribulations also; knowing that tribulation worketh patience (Rom. 5:3).

You see, the thing we glory in, when we go through tribulation, is that our God is victorious over all tribulation.

For He always causes us to triumph (2 Cor. 2:14).

A Bed, a Staff and a Positive Confession

One of the most interesting and amazing parts of Scripture is the record of the Shunammite woman and the death of her son. In this single account God reveals three dynamic faith extenders which this woman employed. The first one is a bed. You may wonder, "How can a bed extend someone's faith?" Well, this was no ordinary bed; it was the bed of the man of God. Read the entire account found in 2 Kings 4:8-37. This bed had been placed there by the Shunammite woman many years earlier, long before it became a life-saving faith extender. She had prepared a room with a bed for the prophet to use when he came into her area. The prophet, wanting to thank her for this kindness, asked her what he could do for her. Her reply was, "I am perfectly content."

After hearing this, the prophet asked his servant, Gehazi, what he thought the woman would like to have. The servant replied, "She has no son and her husband is old." So Elisha said, "Next year, at about this time, you shall have a son!" (2 Kin. 4:16, TLB).

And sure enough, according to the time of life, the next year she had given birth to a son. The next record of the Shunammite's son is given when he has grown up enough to go out with his father to oversee the reapers. Suddenly, the son became very ill with severe pain in his head, and, with the onset of this illness, the father carried him back home to his mother. The Scripture says he lay on her lap until noon and then he died.

Now think carefully. What would be our normal reaction if something like this occurred? We would probably call in an ambulance full of paramedics, then all of our relatives and friends for a time of mourning, and then make funeral arrangements.

But this is not what the Shunammite woman did. She rose up into her most holy faith. She knew God's prophet had power with God and, at that moment, like no other moment in her life, she needed power. For this woman of faith had decided not to accept the decision of death's messenger. When she realized her son was dead, her faith no doubt faltered. But she was determined to stand up to the death angel and deny him that for which he had come. There she stood with the little body in her arms.

The battle raged, but she saw the prophet's bed and remembered all the times that the man of God had lain upon that bed. She immediately placed that little body on the bed. Why, the man of God slept there regularly. His effulgence, no doubt, was upon those bed clothes. Do not scoff at her belief in the power of the effulgence of the man of God. For Scripture relates that when a dead man's body was thrown into the pit that held the bones of Elisha, the dead man came back to life again (2 Kin. 13:21). This bed became a strong faith extender. Notice, though, that she had the wisdom to use another faith extender—her positive confession, "It is well."

> Then she called to her husband, and said, "Please send me one of the young men and one of the donkeys, that I may run to the man of God and come back." So he said, "Why are you going to him today? It is neither the New Moon nor the Sabbath." And she said, "It is well." (2 Kin. 4:22,23, NKJV).

What a statement of faith! Their son was dead, but she boldly said, "It is well." Don't you just know, as she heard herself speaking these faith-filled words, that her faith leaped to an even higher realm. She was simply operating a principle established by her God; she was imitating God.

God...calleth those things which be not as though

they were (Rom. 4:17).

Follow the account as we are introduced to yet another faith extender. As she rides away to get the man of God, Elisha sees her from afar off and sends his servant to ask if all is well with her husband and child (notice that this was not a scheduled visit). Her answer to the servant is, once again, "It is well" (2 Kin. 4:26). Notice how these faith-extending tactics serve her. As she is brought into the presence of the prophet, she does not waver in her faith. She refuses to let fear uproot the faith seeds she had planted. She does not strengthen the death angel's claim on her son by confessing death. Instead, she says, "Did I desire a son of my lord?" (2 Kin. 4:28).

The statement "Did I ask a son of my lord?" at first glance doesn't seem to be a proper greeting. But it is at this point that revelation came to the prophet and, without the woman saying another word, he knew the boy had died. She never had to confess that her son was dead. Her confession remained positive. At this point, the prophet institutes a great faith extender to help keep the faith of the woman high. Hear Elisha as he says to his servant, Gehazi:

> Get yourself ready, and take my staff in your hand and be on your way...lay my staff on the face of the child (2 Kin. 4:29, NKJV).

Elisha sends his staff ahead of him to extend the faith of the woman. She insists that the prophet return with her to her son, but at the same time she knows that his staff will be placed upon the boy even before she returns to him. This kept her faith alive as she traveled back to her home with the prophet.

What a great example of strong faith! This woman used a faith extender from her past—the bed that the prophet had laid on. She used a faith extender in her present situation—her strong positive confession. Even the prophet of God used a faith extender to maintain the woman's strong faith during the journey home. The staff of the man of God lying on that dead corpse was a witness to the woman's faith—faith that was being sparked by the anticipation of the arrival of its owner, the prophet of God. This spark of faith ignited into full power when the prophet arrived at the Shunammite woman's home.

Elisha went into the home where the boy's body lay and closed the door and then prayed to the Lord. After praying and stretching himself upon the dead body, the body became warm and life returned to the boy.

Note: *The writer does not, with the illustration of the Shunammite woman, advocate that a person facing a medical emergency not call an ambulance or paramedics. Each person must make independent emergency decisions.*

Take a moment, as these thoughts are fresh on your mind, and write down a few of your past victories for future use in your arsenal of spiritual weapons. You cannot afford to let the wealth of faith extenders in the Scriptures, and in and around your life, go unnoticed and unused any longer. Keep an eye out for them.

Strong Faith Brings Peace and Tranquility

No amount of worldly motivation can bring forth the peace and tranquility available to those who possess strong faith.

Consider three saints who had this type of strong faith. In the face of the most impossible circumstances, they had faith strong enough to bring forth an abundance of peace and tranquility. The three saints to whom I refer are Shadrach, Meshach and Abednego. These young men had God's principles so firmly established in them that no matter what King Nebuchadnezzar commanded them to do, they would not disobey God. They had such strong faith in their God's power to deliver them that not even the fiery furnace could persuade them to reject God's commandments. Their faith in His ability to deliver them was so great that the Son of God appeared to them, and to their adversaries, in the midst of that fiery furnace.

There isn't any situation from which our great God won't deliver us, if we are obedient to Him and are leaning on Him, instead of on the arm of the flesh.

These three young men had such strong faith because they had exercised and matured it before facing the fiery furnace. How much more easily we could face our fiery furnaces if we could learn how to mature our faith before our trials come, instead of trying to mature it in the midst of them. The three Hebrew children had exercised and matured their faith while in prison, with a powerful faith extender—their diet.

> But Daniel purposed in his heart that he would not defile himself with the portion of the king's meat, nor with the wine which he drank; therefore he requested of the prince of the eunuchs that he might not defile himself (Dan. 1:8).

Each time they ate their special diet, it reminded them that they were not the same people as their heathen captors. With each bite, they were reminded that they and their ancestors were the chosen people of the great God Jehovah. These three young Hebrew men would not defile themselves by eating the king's portion. They had been taught well from God's Word. They didn't want to abandon their beliefs just because they were in forced service to a heathen king. Their God had taught them to abstain from certain meat (Lev. 11:45-47) and never to eat any meat that had been offered to an idol. Since they would not know if any of the meat they were given to eat had been offered to idols, they made the wise decision to abstain from eating any of the king's portion.

This faith extender was not only a direct builder of the faith of these Hebrew children, but also an indirect builder. Everyone who saw them separate themselves from the heathen diet was expecting them to live up to the directives of their God. Their diet was a powerful, constant faith extender. It proved to be very effective when it came time for them to choose between bowing down to an idol with the multitudes or standing firm against the pagan practices with their God. They chose to continue as a peculiar people who would not bow their knee to worship any other god but the true God of Israel.

It is evident that their everyday refusal to participate in the heathen diet to the flesh made it easier for them to reject the heathen diet of idol worship to their spirit.

The peace and tranquility that Shadrach, Meshach and Abednego experienced during their fiery trial is the same kind of peace and tranquility we can experience today as we face our own trials. Praise God! It was the Lord Jesus Himself who met the Hebrew children in the fiery furnace.

How subtle this faith extender of their diet was. But how glorious their deliverance was as God honored strong faith in the face of such great opposition.

CHAPTER SEVEN

Jesus Used Verbalization
As a Faith Extender

"I have overcome the world." This five-word sentence is a classic example of Jesus' speaking of a future event as if it had already happened. Listen to His words in John 16:33:

> These things I have spoken unto you, that in me ye might have peace. In the world ye shall have tribulation: but be of good cheer; I have overcome the world.

What a powerful statement our Lord makes here. There is no hint in any one of these words that this event awaited any future fulfillment. He proclaims it as completed without any further action being needed.

But at the time of this incredible utterance, Jesus had *not yet actually* overcome the world. His complete victory in overcoming the world was still in the future.

I most surely believe the Word of God and I believe it to be infallible. But in John 16:33 we are faced with a dilemma. Jesus clearly says, "I have overcome the world."

The apostle Paul says in Colossians 2:13-15:

> And you, being dead in your sins and the uncircumcision of your flesh, hath he quickened together with him, having forgiven you all trespasses;

> blotting out the handwriting of ordinances that was against us, which was contrary to us, and took it out of the way, nailing it to his cross; and having spoiled principalities and powers, he made a shew of them openly, triumphing over them in it [meaning the cross].

Paul states here that the *actual overcoming* of the world by Jesus took place on the cross of Calvary. The apostle Paul writes in Colossians 2:13-15 that Jesus overcame the world at the time of His death and resurrection. But the statement by Jesus in John 16:33 says, "I *have* overcome the world." This proclamation takes place before His actual death and resurrection. Let's face the question here: Is this a contradiction of fact?

To the natural man, this is a contradiction, but to the spiritual man, there is no contradiction. This is a principle God uses and which He encourages His people to use. Jesus was using the verbalization of a yet-to-happen event as if it *had already happened*. This verbalization expanded and enhanced the faith of His disciples. At the time of our Lord's utterance in John 16:33, He had not yet accomplished the total victory that He boldly declared. This total victory was *actually* accomplished on the cross and in the events surrounding His resurrection.

Only at this point (His death, burial and resurrection) did He once again take total, absolute dominion over all things on this planet—not only on the surface of the planet, but both those things in heaven and on the earth. Only at the moment of the atonement and resurrection did He become victorious in overcoming the world. With all respect to those who teach against the verbalization of the yet unmanifested, I must point out that their strong words against this type of activity went totally unheeded by our Lord. Hear Him as He boldly states in the sixteenth chapter of John, "I have overcome the world."

There are two mentalities inside of you. There is a natural mentality and a spiritual mentality. Your natural mentality thinks like the prince of the powers of the air (Satan). Your spiritual mentality thinks like God.

> God...calleth those things which be not as though they were (Rom. 4:17).

Jesus was simply using God's mindset when He said, "I have overcome the world." In doing so, He verbalized that which was not yet manifested as if it were already completed. He let that mindset be in Him that was in God, even as He tells us to let the mindset of Christ be in us.

> Let this mind be in you, which was also in Christ Jesus (Phil. 2:5).

To understand why Jesus used this faith extender at this particular time, we must understand the statements He had just made to His disciples. Examination of the context reveals that He had just told His disciples there would soon come a time of scattering, a time when they would flee in every direction. But then, with great authority, He tells them not to fear because He had "overcome the world."

Realize that Jesus sensed something in His disciples. He was seeing His revelation of coming events shaking their faith—faith that was rapidly weakening. So He bolstered up their faltering faith with a verbalization of the not yet manifested. Notice He could have said, "And when you are scattered, I plan to overcome the earth." Instead He says, "I have overcome the world." He did this for no other reason than to extend their faith. By His faith in God's ability to keep His Word, He spoke in the present tense of a yet-to-happen event, His total victory over death, hell and the grave, as an already-accomplished event.

Faith is the substance of things hoped for and the

evidence of things not yet seen. His statement was used as a great amplifier for the faith of His disciples, so they could stand on the verbal evidence of that which they could not yet see.

Jesus was doing nothing more than practicing what He preached. It was He who said,

> Whosoever shall say unto this mountain, Be thou removed, and be thou cast into the sea; and shall not doubt in his heart, but shall believe that those things which he saith shall come to pass; he shall have whatsoever he saith (Mark 11:23).

In the saying of "Be thou removed," the Lord is not speaking of the mountain being removed some day. But He was speaking of its present state of being removed and cast into the sea.

The "seed" of Jesus' victory over the world was planted by God before the foundation of the world. Jesus was merely watering it with His positive words of faith. "You shall have whatsoever you say."

I hope you are grounded firmly enough in Bible knowledge to know that words are powerful. The Bible says that words have within them the power of life and death.

> Death and life are in the power of the tongue; and they that love it shall eat the fruit thereof (Prov. 18:21).

What a strange series of events! One day Jesus declares, "I have overcome the world." But no more than a few days later we see Him at the mercy of the world, dying a shameful death, being ridiculed, spit upon, laughed at and reviled by the weakest and lowest of people. Then this One, who had just days before declared, "I have overcome the world," was sealed into a borrowed tomb.

Granted, there is something here that sets off an alarm

in the *natural* mind. But, thank God, through the power of the new birth, we have access to renewed spiritual minds—the mind of Christ. The spiritual mind grasps this series of events not as a contradiction but simply as the way God speaks.

Your spiritual man will be trained to know the ways of God, if you constantly expose it to the Word.

For my thoughts are not your thoughts [natural thoughts], neither are your ways my ways [natural ways], saith the Lord (Is. 55:8).

As I travel the world, I am seeing something so very wonderful. There is a new kind of Christian appearing in every nation. He (I speak of both men and women) is attempting to *imitate Jesus* by speaking those things that are not, as if they already were.

If Jesus used this kind of faith extender while He was on earth, shouldn't we also take advantage of this powerful spiritual weapon? The answer is an emphatic yes. I encourage you to begin today to speak, by faith, of your pending victories as already accomplished. Speak your God-given goals as though they were already attained.

For instance, if your present spiritual battle is to stop smoking, don't continue to speak of *"when* I quit smoking!" Say boldly, "I have quit smoking!"

If you desire a closer walk with God by an increased prayer life, drop that old "I wish I could pray more" line. Stop saying, "When I start praying more powerfully." We know it takes strong faith to accomplish the goal of a strong prayer life. It is also common knowledge that your faith is greatly hindered by non-committed, wishful speaking. Why not just do as Jesus did and speak out that your prayer life *is* becoming more powerful and effective every day? This will work in almost every circumstance of your life.

This simple but powerful faith extender, the speaking

of things yet unmanifested as though they were already manifested, will begin to strengthen, extend and magnify your faith. Allow your faith to reach beyond the numerous limitations of the natural realm into the possibilities of the supernatural realm.

When Jesus Cleansed the Temple

To understand the actions of Jesus in the cleansing of the temple, you must understand that He cleansed the temple *twice*. In three of the Gospels, we read about the cleansing of the temple that took place just before He went to the cross.

> And he went into the temple, and began to cast out them that sold therein, and them that bought; saying unto them, It is written, My house is the house of prayer: but ye have made it a den of thieves (Luke 19:45,46).

(The other two Scripture passages follow this same general wording and are found in Matthew 21:10-13 and Mark 11:15-17.)

There is, however, another cleansing of the temple, separate from the cleansing that occurred right before His death. The apostle John records it. This was the first cleansing of the temple, and it occurred at the beginning of Jesus' ministry. In this account we read:

> After this he went down to Capernaum, he, and his mother, and his brethren, and his disciples: [He had just come from turning the water into wine] and they continued there not many days. And the Jews' passover was at hand, and Jesus went up to Jerusalem, and found in the temple those that sold oxen and sheep and doves, and the changers of money sitting: And when he had made a scourge of small

cords, he drove them all out of the temple, and the sheep, and the oxen; and poured out the changers' money, and overthrew the tables; and said unto them that sold doves, Take these things hence; make not my Father's house an house of merchandise. And His disciples remembered that it was written, The zeal of thine house hath eaten me up. Then answered the Jews and said unto him, What sign shewest thou unto us, seeing that thou doest these things? Jesus answered and said unto them, Destroy this temple, and in three days I will raise it up. Then said the Jews, Forty and six years was this temple in building, and wilt thou rear it up in three days? But he spake of the temple of his body (John 2:12-21).

When Jesus entered the Jerusalem temple to cleanse it, He was not emphasizing the necessity of cleaning up some stone buildings (religious shrines) that the Jews had long since perverted. He was illustrating to those in the temple and to all those who would read of the account throughout the following ages, those who have the spirit of revelation, that we must clean up our own temples (our bodies). He is emphasizing that we must use strong discipline to drive wrong attitudes and perversions from our lives. We must overturn the tables of self-righteousness and pride that infest our temples. We must chase the merchants (those things that would make merchandise of our souls) and the animals of our carnal nature and demonic influences out the doors and windows of our souls and spirits. We must exercise strong, sometimes even harsh, discipline upon the intruders who attempt to establish strongholds in our own temples.

If we are going to have our temple be a fit dwelling place for God, we're going to have to get tough with our old man and the lingering influence of his old nature. The Scripture is clear in John 2:21. It states that Jesus was referring to the temple of His own body, not the stone temple that men took some forty-six years to build. This great, illustrated teaching—a faith extender—should etch itself upon our minds. It should motivate us to keep our bodies (the temples of God) purged from intruders. What a graphic illustration and great faith builder.

But remember, although we must be strong in cleansing and disciplining our own temple, we must be merciful and loving when disciplining others. We must follow the example of the patterned Son, Jesus, and show love, kindness and grace when we see the shortcomings of others. We are taught to cleanse our own temple, not our brother's temple.

From the first time I received the revelation of this truth, it has ever been before me. When I deal with others, I must be sweet and gentle. When I deal with myself, I must get rough.

The apostle Paul perpetuates this teaching when he speaks of "bringing his body into subjection."

> But I keep under my body, and bring in into subjection: lest that by any means, when I have preached to others, I myself should be a castaway (1 Cor. 9:27).

There is no question, upon the reading of this account, but that the apostle Paul got rough with himself when he dealt with disciplining his body.

When the Lord cleansed the temple, He was showing us that we need to cleanse our temples on a regular basis. Sometimes this cleansing takes place by the Word (which is commonly called the "water"), and other times we must make up a scourge of spiritual "cords" and go into our own inner temple and clean house! We must not allow the merchants of carnality, gossip, lying, cheating, evil imaginations and the like, to set up shop in our temple. We are each responsible for the cleansing of our own temple, just as Jesus was for His.

> I beseech you therefore, brethren, by the mercies of God, that ye present your bodies a living sacrifice, holy, acceptable unto God, which is your reasonable service (Rom. 12:1).

I challenge you to take up this illustration. Do the same thing with your body as Jesus did with the Jerusalem temple. Clean it out! Walk in and shout, "All you thieves and robbers, moneychangers and evil spirits—get out! Out! My body is the temple of the God Jehovah and He insists on its being clean."

Remember, Scripture admonishes us that after thoroughly cleansing the temple of our body, we must fill it properly.

> When the unclean spirit is gone out of a man, he walketh through dry places, seeking rest, and findeth none. Then he saith, I will return into my house from whence I came out; and when he is come, he findeth it empty, swept and garnished. Then goeth he, and taketh with himself seven other spirits more wicked than himself, and they enter in and dwell there: and the last state of that man is worse than the first. Even so shall it be also unto this wicked generation (Matt. 12:43-45).

Being filled with the Holy Ghost and staying filled with the Holy Ghost assures a minimum of house cleaning. As we have already mentioned, we are to make kindness, love and grace our bywords as we minister to others. Let's also remember to get tough with ourselves! Your old man is Jacob (the supplanter). He is the one person with whom you have to get rough and to whom you must lay down the law. If you are too easy on yourself, that old nature will overrun and ruin your temple. You simply won't get the job of cleansing done with a light hand. Your old man doesn't understand easy treatment and gentleness—he'll take advantage of it!

The ability to grow strong faith does not lie in our great intelligence, nor does it lie in our great theological and philosophical expertise. Rather it lies in our willingness and ability to understand and accept God's Word and His purposes for our life. What better way is there to achieve that understanding than to have our faith expanded and extended with faith extenders?

CHAPTER EIGHT

Jesus Used Anticipation
As a Faith Extender

The Bible is full of illustrations of faith being stimulated by anticipation. Anticipation stimulators can greatly serve us to amplify and strengthen our faith. They are legitimate weapons to use in our daily spiritual warfare. Remember:

> For the weapons of our warfare are not carnal; but mighty through God to the pulling down of strongholds (2 Cor. 10:4).

They Saved the Best Wine for Last

In the turning of water to wine, Jesus used anticipation as an expander of faith. John 2:1-11 records the account of the first miracle that Jesus performed during His visit to the marriage feast at Cana of Galilee:

> The third day there was a marriage in Cana of Galilee; and the mother of Jesus was there. And both Jesus was called, and his disciples, to the marriage. And when they [the guests] wanted wine, the mother of Jesus saith unto him, They have no wine. Jesus saith unto her, Woman, what have I to do with thee? Mine hour is not yet come. His mother saith unto the servants, Whatsoever he saith unto you, do it. And there were set there six waterpots of

stone...[The context seems to indicate that He requested them] (John 2:1-6).

Can't you almost hear the dialogue that took place. The servants standing by were saying, "What are you going to do with the waterpots, Jesus?"

The context seems to indicate that, in the beginning of the discussion, Jesus was quite non-committal. But when He instructed the servants, Jesus might have answered them this way, "I am going to turn this water into wine."

The servants no doubt said, "If you are making wine, shouldn't it be done in wineskins? Because wine goes into wineskins, not into waterpots."

His response to them probably would have been, "I understand that wine most certainly goes into wineskins—but those standing about me can't see into a wineskin. For wineskins have such small pouring holes in them (about the diameter of a pencil). They are too small for a man to look into. Besides that, it's dark in a wineskin and no one can see inside it. I want everyone here to see the water and what is happening to it. I want them to mix their anticipation with My faith. I want the necessary ingredient of faith to be present." The necessary ingredient of faith that Jesus spoke of here was anticipation (the thing hoped for).

Now faith is the substance of things hoped for, the evidence of things not seen (Heb. 11:1).

So He used waterpots with wide brims. Notice that He had them filled to the top (for the best viewing). With this, He hoped to stimulate the greatest anticipation possible from the spectators. His desire was to bring their faith to His faith's level. He wanted an atmosphere of strong faith to fill that entire gathering, as they participated in the miracle. Picture the anticipation charged atmosphere. Surely it would be most conducive to accomplishing the miracle. Remember how the working of mighty miracles was hindered in Jesus' home city of Nazareth when unbelief and lack of anticipation stopped the mighty works.

And he did not many mighty works there [Nazareth] because of their unbelief (Matt. 13:58).

Now with all this in mind, view the scene with new eyes. See the waterpots, with their wide brims filled to the top with clear water. Don't you just know that the mere sight of these massive pots, with Jesus standing before them, must have started anticipation rising in their midst? Let me suggest what may have been said as the servants and disciples stood there: "Is He really going to try to turn ordinary water into wine? Hey, move over! Let me see." (The anticipation was building.)

"Why, He means business. He is really going to try to do it!" When anticipation is at its highest level, Jesus brings forth the miracle with the words: "Draw out now, and bear unto the governor of the feast" (John 2:8).

Although it was His "first miracle," He did not say, "Draw out to let me taste first to see if the water is now wine." This statement would have questioned whether the miracle had been performed or not. But, without hesitation, He had the first-drawn cupful brought to the governor of the feast. As saints of God, we are to have the same kind of faith—faith that does not question our right to perform the supernatural.

Think of how quickly we would turn this planet upside-down, if believers would learn the secret of using the faith extender of anticipation.

Picture an auditorium full of believers, arriving hours before a healing crusade. See these early-comers taking seats up front, hours before the first sick person came. Picture them sitting there, full of anticipation, praying, believing, expecting total victory as they await the visitation of God in the meeting. This kind of atmosphere would be conducive to manifold miracles!

Think with me again. This time picture a drought-stricken community standing at the brink of famine, as the saints of God plan a "last resort" prayer meeting. They must have immediate rain. They declare that the prayer meeting will commence at a set hour, at the top of the hill, just outside of town. The sole objective of this meeting is to pray down an immediate rainstorm. Every saint in the community is recruited and committed to come to the hilltop with their faith in its strongest order. This will be a do-or-die effort.

Can you imagine how much power it would add to that prayer meeting if rain was anticipated? Just imagine all those would-be prayer warriors who did not already have raincoats and galoshes out frantically trying to buy them before the prayer meeting begins. Picture them as they descend upon the local clothing stores to buy every rain-coat, every pair of rubber boots and every umbrella in town! Can't you just imagine how the faith level around that town would rise, if those saints, who could not find rain gear to buy, were to go out among the unbelievers and borrow their raincoats and umbrellas? They would be clearly stating to these unbelievers that they were prepar-ing for the rainstorm their pending prayer meeting would surely generate. Why, the whole town would be buzzing with anticipation, if, hours before the appointed time of the drought-breaking prayer meeting, the saints were closing up their windows, taking wash down from the clotheslines, replacing worn windshield wipers at the local filling stations and putting fresh washer fluid in their wind-shield washers.

Then imagine the saints congregating on the hilltop, every one of them fully suited up for a rainstorm. Um-brellas are opening over that hillside until it resembles a mushroom-covered knoll. Would this strengthen or weaken the faith of the saints? I say it would strengthen their faith. It would even cause the faith of the non-believer to stir. Without a doubt, it would greatly amplify, multiply, extend and intensify everyone's faith. With the stir of preparation, anticipation would rise and strong faith would be manifested.

I believe that, if we can cause a hindering mountain to be cast into the sea, as instructed in Scripture, we can most surely speak in this same faith to the drought-stricken sky and cause it to bring forth an abundance of rain. Strong faith can move even the mountain of drought.

When the church operates in the realm of strong faith— faith which has been magnified to its most powerful state— needs, and even wants, will be easily supplied by God. I include wants because the miracle of the turning of water into wine was, by no stretch of the imagination, classified as a simple meeting of the necessities of the wedding guests. But fine wine would be a luxury. We clearly see here, in the first miracle of Jesus, His approval of wants.

Anointing for Jesus' Burial

Consider an incident that took place in the life of Jesus when He encouraged the acting out of an event before it took place. This event was a powerful faith extender of anticipation. This was such an important event that the woman who enacted it received the highest of commendations and reward from our Lord Jesus.

And being in Bethany in the house of Simon the leper, as he sat at meat, there came a woman having an alabaster box of ointment of spikenard very precious; and she brake the box, and poured it on his head. And there were some that had indignation

within themselves, and said, Why was this waste
of the ointment made? For it might have been sold
for more than three hundred pence, and have been
given to the poor. And they murmured against her.
And Jesus said, Let her alone; why trouble ye her?
She hath wrought a good work on me. For ye have
the poor with you always, and whensoever ye will
ye may do them good; but me ye have not always.
She hath done what she could: she is come afore-
hand to anoint my body to the burying. Verily I say
unto you, Wheresoever this gospel shall be preached
throughout the whole world, this also that she hath
done shall be spoken of for a memorial of her (Mark
14:3-9).

It was unheard of to anoint a person for burial before
his death. Rather the accepted practice was to anoint the
body after death. But notice that Jesus did not stop her;
rather He allowed her to complete the entire procedure.
Afterwards, He quickly let all who had witnessed this
premature anointing know that she had done a good thing.
She had come to draw attention to His imminent death with
a pre-death anointing of His body. Therefore, He said to
let her proceed without hindrance of complaint. She did
just that, picturing, through the anointing of His body, that
soon Jesus would die.

Jesus allowed this pre-enactment of the anointing of His
soon-to-be-dead body to impress the fact of His coming
death upon the minds of the disciples. He did this so that
when they saw Him die, their faith would not collapse
totally. He wanted them to know that everything was going according to plan and nothing had gone wrong. But,
as we all know, the disciples, to a man, supposed that all
was lost when they saw Him dead on the cross. Strange
as it may seem, with so many references by Jesus to His

death and resurrection, all of His disciples lost faith at the time of His death by crucifixion. In facing His dead body, even after the strongest of faith extenders, they still did not believe. Now it seemed as if His words and pictures of His death were futile. But there came a time, after His resurrection, that those words of His resurrection and the faith extender of the pre-death anointing ignited the faith of His disciples.

> He is not here, but is risen: remember how he spake unto you when he was yet in Galilee, Saying, The Son of man must be delivered into the hands of sinful men, and be crucified, and the third day rise again. And they remembered his words (Luke 24:6-8).

> These things understood not his disciples at the first: but when Jesus was glorified, then remembered they that these things were written of him, and that they had done these things unto him (John 12:16).

"Receive Ye the Holy Ghost"

Probably the most graphic faith builder that Jesus ever used is illustrated in John 20:19. Those of you who even lightly study theology know that theologians throughout history have a problem with this passage. Jesus makes this statement:

> Then the same day at evening, being the first day of the week, when the doors were shut where the disciples were assembled for fear of the Jews, came Jesus and stood in the midst, and saith unto them, Peace be unto you. And when he had so said, he shewed unto them his hands and his side. Then were the disciples glad, when they saw the Lord. Then said Jesus to them again, Peace be unto you: as my

Father hath sent me, even so send I you. And when
he had said this, he breathed on them, and saith unto
them, Receive ye the Holy Ghost (John 20:19-22).

Let me sketch briefly the theological problem created
here by this statement of Jesus. It is common knowledge
that the Holy Ghost was given on the day of Pentecost.
How then could Jesus give the Holy Ghost before His
ascension and before that marvelous manifestation of the
Holy Ghost in the second chapter of Acts?

We read in Acts 1:4-8 that they were to tarry in the city
of Jerusalem, and not many days would pass until the Holy
Ghost would come to them and they would receive unusual
power. Then, in the second chapter of Acts, we see the
source of that power, the Holy Ghost, and how that power
displayed itself as a mighty rushing wind.

From John 20:19-22, we understand what Jesus was
actually saying to them: "Beloved, I want you to be prepared to receive the Holy Ghost." When He breathed on
them a breath of air, it illustrated to them that when the
Holy Spirit came, His coming would be accompanied by
the sound of a mighty wind. Weeks later, when the Holy
Ghost was given on the day of Pentecost, He arrived with
the sound of a mighty, rushing wind.

And suddenly there came a sound from heaven as
of a rushing mighty wind, and it filled all the house
where they were sitting (Acts 2:2).

As the sound of a mighty wind was heard, they grasped
what was happening. Why? Because their great God had
already rehearsed this blessed moment with them, complete with the sound of wind, some forty days before. He
had already acted out this experience earlier as He blew
His breath upon them, giving them a very graphic foretaste
of what was to come. Every time they heard the wind blow
during those forty days, their faith grew. The anticipation

of the coming of the Holy Spirit came with every sound of rushing wind. With faith made strong by anticipation and increased with each sound of wind, they were well prepared to recognize and receive the dynamic outpouring of God's Spirit. As their faith responded, they were empowered on the day of Pentecost with power to be witnesses in Jerusalem, Judea, Samaria and the uttermost parts of the world.

These men, without theological knowledge or understanding, were able to grasp this great spiritual truth. In the days that followed, these simple laymen, taught by simple illustrations, brought forth the most powerful words ever written by man. How could these simple men possibly bring forth documents like the four Gospels? Because they had learned the wisdom of the ages by simple illustrations.

Today, the growing of strong faith in us does not lie in our great intelligence. Neither does it lie in our great theological and philosophical expertise. Rather it lies in our willingness and ability to understand and accept God's Word and His purposes for our life. What better way is there to achieve that understanding than by having our faith expanded and extended with faith extenders like this one: Our Lord's blowing on His disciples prepared them to associate the sound of rushing wind with the appearing of the Holy Ghost.

Spittle and Mud Make a Vivid Faith Extender

Now let's focus our attention on a very earthy faith extender. Our Lord, in this instance, uses spittle mixed with the dust to make a unique faith extender. This wonderful faith extender appears in the ninth chapter of John.

And as Jesus passed by, he saw a man which was blind from his birth. And his disciples asked him,

93

saying, Master, who did sin, this man, or his parents, that he was born blind? Jesus answered, Neither hath this man sinned, nor his parents: but that the works of God should be made manifest in him. I must work the works of him that sent me, while it is day: the night cometh, when no man can work. As long as I am in the world, I am the light of the world. When he had thus spoken, he spat on the ground, and made clay of the spittle, and he anointed the eyes of the blind man with the clay. And said unto him, Go, wash in the pool of Siloam, (which is by interpretation, Sent). He went his way therefore, and washed, and came seeing (John 9:1-7).

The King James Version of the Bible says simply, "He anointed the eyes." Other translations of the Bible read as follows: "He smeared clay over the eyes" (Weymouth). "He dabbed the mud on his eyes" (Berkley). "He smoothed the mud over the blind man's eyes" (the Living Bible). "He spread the clay upon his eyes" (New English and Amplified versions). Notice how the modern translations show us more perfectly what Jesus did.

The full impact of what happened is not realized until we understand that this was not merely a ceremonial anointing, but, as the margin of many Bibles indicates, it was a *spreading* of the clay over the eyes. Ordinarily, spreading clay on one's eyes would be an irritant. Even a small amount of clay and spittle rubbed into the eye would be extremely annoying. All of us, at one time or another, have had a "speck" of something in our eyes. If you are like me, you have found it very discomforting.

But Jesus packed mud over the man's eyes, making clay blinders over his eyes. Even a man who could see would be unable to see if he had thick shields of mud over his eyes. After applying these mud shields, Jesus told the blind man to go and wash in the pool of Siloam and then he would be able to see.

With the mud shields over his eyes, the man's inability to see could no longer be blamed on his non-functioning eyes. Now there was a physical obstacle between his eyes and the outside world. He felt his way along the path that led to the pool. He did not feel for his way because of non-functioning eyes, but because of mud shields over his eyes. His faith grew stronger with each step as he now faced the simple task of washing off mud blinders, instead of the impossible task of seeing with blind eyes.

During the entire trip to the pool of Siloam, he could focus his faith on his healing, without the constant darkness of those non-functioning eyes to destroy his faith. His faith could soar. He could believe that his eyes were healed. He could imagine the light of day streaming through as the water of the pool would soon be washing away those mud blinders. He could now add the faith extender of anticipation to his faith.

The man needed only to get his mind off the hopelessness of his blind condition for healing faith to arise. In just a little while, the obstructions to his sight would be gone from his eyes and he would see the glorious light of day.

That was an anticipation-filled moment as the mud shields dissolved in the clear water of the pool. Why, he had washed mud off his body many times and the result was always the same—as soon as the water was applied to the mud, it quickly dissolved. Now he could easily visualize the water dissolving the clay barrier and removing it so his newly healed eyes could see. As he opened his eyelids, which had been shut by the weight of the mud shields, faith was pushed upward as anticipation peaked. No one knows how long the blinders were on. They may have been on as long as a half hour. However long it was, one thing was certain—his eyes couldn't bring forth their faith-destroying testimony of blindness! They could already be healed. There could be, lying just beneath those cool mud packs, eyes that could see with the keenest of vision.

For the first time, the blindness couldn't prove itself. Minute by minute, his faith grew. Hear his inner voice as it proclaims, "It's almost gone. The clay is almost washed away. Just another moment and I'm going to be able to see." And when the clay was gone and he opened his eyes—glory to God!—he could see!

I believe that Jesus healed this man as He did others— according to the man's faith.

> And, behold, there came a leper and worshipped him, saying, Lord, if thou wilt, thou canst make me clean....As thou hast believed, so be it done unto thee (Matt. 8:2,13).

> Then touched he their [blind men's] eyes, saying, according to your faith be it unto you (Matt. 9:29).

> Then Jesus answered and said unto her, O woman, great is thy faith: be it unto thee even as thou wilt (Matt. 15:28).

Please notice that I am in no way attempting to explain away the miracles that Jesus most surely performed. My only intention here is to show how the faith extender that Jesus used amplified and expanded the blind man's faith. This faith extender heightened anticipation and hindered the blind eyes from witnessing contrary to the testimony of God. It made it easier for the man to receive that which Jesus willingly provided.

The disciples learned from Jesus' example. Let me illustrate. When Simon Peter was called to Joppa to witness the death of Tabitha (Acts 9:36-41), notice carefully that he would not allow himself to look at her dead body before he spoke the words of resurrection life to her. The Bible states, "Peter...turning...to the body said, Tabitha, arise" (Acts 9:40).

Peter let his faith build before he spoke. He refused to look at her dead corpse. He didn't allow its stark, cold, lifeless testimony to weaken his faith.

I have been in the room in Joppa where Tabitha lay dead. If he had to turn about to see her, then his back was to the body. If his back was to the body, his face would have had to be looking out the window at the teeming life on the docks just below her window.

Simon Peter, by not looking at the body, refused to let the dead body build a case against his faith in her resurrection. Instead, he let his faith grow stronger and stronger, looking at the life outside the window. Then, with the strongest of faith, he turned himself about and rebuked death before it could rebuke his faith. As the account in Acts states, Tabitha was raised from the dead.

Never lose sight of the importance of protecting your faith from unbelief. For unbelief stops the works of God. But faith releases the supply of God.

According to your faith be it unto you (Matt. 9:29).

Not only does faith release God's provision to us, but our lack of faith greatly stops the miracle-working power of God in our midst.

Anything that minimizes the forces of doubt and unbelief is a great faith extender!

CHAPTER NINE

Jesus Used Possibility Thinking As a Faith Extender

Miracle of the Loaves and Fishes

Another excellent example of the scriptural use of faith extenders is well illustrated in the miracle of the loaves and fishes.

> After these things Jesus went over the sea of Galilee, which is the sea of Tiberias. And a great multitude followed him, because they saw his miracles which he did on them that were diseased. And Jesus went up into a mountain, and there he sat with his disciples. And the passover, a feast of the Jews, was nigh. When Jesus then lifted up his eyes, and saw a great company come unto him, he saith unto Philip, Whence shall we buy bread, that these may eat? (John 6:1-5).

Jesus begins solving the problem by bringing attention to the fact that a natural solution is highly improbable. Follow the context very carefully. First, Jesus asks a question, "Where are we going to buy enough bread to feed all of these people?"

> And this he said to prove him [Philip]: for he himself knew what he would do (John 6:6).

Jesus already had His mind made up as to what He was going to do. The whole exercise that followed was for the benefit of those who were with Him. He took advantage of a chance to exercise their possibility thinking.

With this question, two very diverse thinking patterns emerge. The scriptural account shows two patterns of thinking and gives space to both. I believe they were both given space for a good reason, to show the dramatic contrast in the way these two conclusions are structured. They approach the situation of the hungry multitude in different ways.

This was an enormous problem. There were 5,000 men, plus women and children—probably 15,000 to 20,000 hungry people, who needed to eat. These people were too hungry and weak to walk to the city and eat. The *impossibility thinker*'s view was amply represented by Philip. His view of the situation was typical of this world's impossibility thinkers. When Philip reached for a solution, he reached into his natural mind. This solution took into account only the realm of the visible, which, as always, is full of impossibilities. His natural mind could not see beyond the obstacles. All he could see was the huge crowd and the magnitude of their need. Philip was held captive by the impossibility of the circumstances. His God-given imagination was so overwhelmed and busy with the impossibilities of the natural that it blocked out the myriad possibilities in the supernatural.

Let's examine Philip's thought process. Hear him as he reasons, "Two hundred pennyworth of bread is not sufficient to meet this astronomical need. It will just not be sufficient, no matter how small we portion it out." Hear unbelief, as it fortifies the stubborn presence of the curse, "There is not enough." How deflating these words were to his faith, and how they multiplied and fortified the doctrine of the kingdom of darkness. This doctrine says,

"There isn't enough." Just listen to the harsh solution that impossibility thinking spawns.

> Send the multitude away, that they may go into the villages and buy themselves victuals (Matt. 14:15).

Impossibility thinking says, "Two hundred pennyworth of bread is not enough. Send them away! There is not enough!"

This is the sum total of the mind of the impossibility thinker. The solutions of the impossibility thinker will always quench faith. Any prolonged exposure to their negative solutions will drain all the reserve power from the batteries of faith. Negative words of insufficiency are especially destructive when they come from the mouths of the sons and daughters of God. For God's Word states that we serve the God of *all sufficiency*.

Now hear the crisp, clean sound of a *possibility thinker* as Andrew (Simon Peter's brother) declares a striking contrast to that which Philip had so graphically and gloomily articulated. Andrew approaches Jesus with a faith-sparked, possibility-filled comment:

> There is a lad here, which hath five barley loaves, and two small fishes (John 6:9).

Andrew demonstrates the possibility thinker. He responded like Mary, the mother of Jesus, at the wedding feast, when she says, "Whatever He (Jesus) says, do it." Andrew saw possibility in a few fish and loaves in the hands of Jesus. He felt that the need for a solution outweighed the problem. He focused on what they had instead of what they lacked. They had two fish. They had five loaves. Now I must admit that his faith was under attack. His next words tell us he must have heard Philip's rehearsal of the impossibilities when he says, "But what are they among so many?"

Please notice the thin line that exists between possibility thinking and impossibility thinking. One of the disciples in effect said, "There is nothing we can do for a crowd as large as this. All the money we have and more would not buy enough bread to feed this many people."

The other disciple speaks to the same problem, but with the optimism of possibility thinking. He focuses on the ability of Jesus to do something with that little boy's lunch. Now keep in mind that he was aware of the problem. He said there were very many people. But, instead of focusing on the impossibility of the situation, he chose to focus his attention on what Jesus could do with what was in the little boy's hand. He knew who Jesus was. With no doubt in his mind, he thought, "I've seen Jesus do powerful and miraculous things before with the smallest, most insignificant beginnings." He had seen Him make wine out of common water. Can't you see how Andrew's possibility thinking nourished the faith of all who heard him?

It doesn't take any imagination to recognize the shortages and shortcomings of a given situation and give up or bring forth an expensive solution. Any impossibility thinker can solve the problem of an overcrowded church auditorium by building a new, multi-million-dollar auditorium. However, it takes a possibility thinker to see all of the possibilities that will solve a problem, along with the impossibilities. The possibility thinker immediately sees the old auditorium serving twice as many people through rearranging the seating, redesigning the platform, removing a wall, putting in a balcony or going to multiple services. Any one of these creative ideas has the possibility of doubling the present capacity of the church. A combination of several of them could even triple or quadruple the seating capacity. The ability to think of the possibility of any given situation is a definite faith extender. With possibilities comes hope, and hope is one of the things the

Bible says faith is.

> Now faith is the substance of things hoped for, the
> evidence of things not seen (Heb. 11:1).

Let your imagination run with this next thought. Hear
the Master as He asks, "How are we going to feed this
crowd? How will we feed the gospel to Africa, India,
China and the rest of the world?" What is your answer?
Is it "Well, Lord, a billion dollars can't do the job. It's
too big!" As you speak these words, feel the strength run
out of your faith.

But if we answer as Andrew answered, "Lord, here is
a printing press. Lord, I know where there is a radio sta-
tion for sale. Lord, how about television? Could we use
television? Could we begin by sending some missionaries?
Maybe we could train the nationals." How quickly our
faith increases at the sound of possibility thinking.

Catch this truth. There is no comparison of the two solutions in the natural. The possibility thinker's solution was
inadequate. Philip's solution of buying 200 pennyworth
of bread made much more sense. While it wouldn't be
nearly enough, at least it would show that their hearts were
in the right place.

Seeing the impossibilities is not a bad thing. The real
man or woman of faith sees the impossibilities. Those who
walk by faith do not walk unrealistically. What they do,
however, is choose to walk in a superior realm of the
Spirit. Before any miracle can be called forth, we must
determine God's will in the solution of the problem.

> And this is the confidence that we have in him, that,
> if we ask any thing according to his will, he heareth
> us: And if we know that he hear us, whatsoever
> we ask, we know that we have the petitions that we
> desired of him (1 John 5:14,15).

Agreement comes into play with the possibility solution that Andrew introduces. There were at least two who had faith in the boy's lunch as a solution. No doubt the little boy who had volunteered his lunch had the full expectation that it would weigh heavily in the solution of the problem. The boy had faith even though the two fish and five loaves were as nothing in the face of 15,000 hungry people. Andrew felt that, in the hands of Jesus, the little lunch basket offering would be carried past the natural realm of its limited possibilities into the supernatural realm. In this realm, even the smallest possibility takes on limitless possibilities.

A second thing the boy's offering had going for it was that the little boy knew Andrew had power with God. Andrew had access to Jesus. When that little boy put his offering into the hands of God's man, it was safe from the peril of being wasted. You see, if the boy had placed that offering in the wrong hands, it would have come to naught. If he had given it to someone who acted like a leader but had no influence with Jesus, his offering might have simply been eaten by the imposter. It would have met the imposter's need but never reached the multitudes' need. Always be careful with your offering, to plant it only in the good ground. Know the ministries to which you give.

Let me show you more clearly how the little boy's lunch was used to extend faith. See Jesus placing the loaves and fishes in a basket and praying over them. Surely He thanked God for the little boy's faith, then for Andrew's faith to bring the boy and his lunch to Him. No doubt He rehearsed to the Father His promise of supply when the conditions of agreement are met.

> Again I say unto you, That if two of you shall agree
> on earth as touching any thing that they shall ask,
> it shall be done for them of my Father which is

in heaven (Matt. 18:19).

Then Jesus broke apart that which was in the basket. Each time He broke off a piece, He would pass it out among the disciples for distribution to the people. I am sure that God did not immediately dump tons of fish and bread in a great heap all around the Lord; rather, bit by bit, piece by piece, there was more and more fish in the basket.

What was the faith extender in this miracle? Before the fish and bread were brought forth, the multitudes had hundreds of ideas in their heads as to what they would like to eat. But notice that when the fish and bread were in the Lord's hands, there came a focusing and agreement as to what would be multiplied. It was going to be fish and bread. Look again at Matthew 18:19 and see how important agreement is.

A second great faith extender is seen in the basket of fish. Once again, as with the turning of water into wine, heightened anticipation came into play, expanding the faith of the disciples. They had seen this same sort of miracle before. It had happened when Jesus stood over the waterpots preparing to meet the desires of those at the wedding feast at Cana of Galilee.

"Ah," you might say, "how much difference could there be in the strength of the disciples' faith as they prayed over an empty basket, or if they prayed over a partially filled basket?" Well, on a scale of one to ten, I don't know how to score it. But I do know that there doesn't have to be much increase of faith to do the mighty works of God. Faith only as a mustard seed will move mountains. So any degree of increase in faith is a tremendous increase.

Without a doubt, Jesus could have done things differently. He could have had the people sit in neat little groups and caused food like manna to fall from the sky. He could have performed any number of mighty miracles completely on His own, without involving the disciples. But He desired that His disciples learn how to face their problems with possibility thinking. He was teaching them how to work *with* God instead of only having God work for them. The disciples learned this lesson.

They went forth, and preached every where, the Lord working with them (Mark 16:20).

God has demonstrated that He does not wish to move independently of man. He wishes to include man in the great work of faith, as together with Him we set out to win the world in these last days.

Catch the purpose behind all of this: He used the bread and fish as focal points for faith and as focal points of anticipation for the miracle. Notice that the loaves and fishes uniquely represented both the need and the solution. Both conditions were represented in that basket. The need was hunger, caused by a lack of food. The solution was food to satisfy the hunger. The initial five loaves and two fishes were, as I call them, faith extenders.

CHAPTER TEN

Faith Extenders Throughout The New Testament

There is no more graphic illustration in Scripture of a closed door being opened than the account of Simon Peter in Herod's prison.

> Now about that time Herod the king stretched forth his hands to vex certain of the church. And he killed James the brother of John with the sword. And because he saw it pleased the Jews, he proceeded further to take Peter also. (Then were the days of unleavened bread.) And when he had apprehended him, he put him in prison, and delivered him to four quaternions of soldiers to keep him; intending after Easter to bring him forth to the people. Peter therefore was kept in prison: but prayer was made without ceasing of the church unto God for him. And when Herod would have brought him forth, the same night Peter was sleeping between two soldiers, bound with two chains; and the keepers before the door kept the prison (Acts 12:1-6).

Verses 1-3 above clearly show that it was the intention of King Herod to kill Peter as he had killed James, the brother of John. But Simon Peter, full of faith, calmly laid down between the two guards and fell sound asleep in faith—strong faith. These terrifying circumstances would

107

have quickly obliterated weak faith. Peter, however, rested in faith. He knew those iron gates were of a lesser strength than his God's ability to deliver him.

Faith Is the Key

You see, faith is the key. It unlocks any door that stands between you and God's perfect supply of your needs and wants. Remember, it is not tradition or folklore, but it is the Scriptures that tell us if we say to the mountain, ''Be thou removed, and be thou cast into the sea; and shall not doubt in his heart, [believing in our heart, without doubt of any kind], but shall believe that those things which he saith shall come to pass; he shall have whatsoever he saith [it will happen exactly as we say]'' (Mark 11:23).

The removing of any mountain is as great a task as originally placing the mountain where it now stands. The informed child of God knows how the mountains got where they are today. They were spoken by faith into place from their pre-creation, invisible state into their now-visible state by God. Hebrews 11 tells us that the raw material that mountains are made of is faith. So if a mountain is to be removed and cast into the sea, it will have to be moved by the same power that placed it originally in the mountain range. Faith is as powerful in the bringing forth of desired things as it is in the removing of undesirable things.

A Good Night's Sleep—a Faith Preserver

How greatly the circumstances had changed when Simon Peter awoke. With his awakening, he found the fetters that bound him fallen away, sleeping guards at his side and the prison door wide open. Notice the faith extender that was either consciously or subconsciously used by Simon Peter. He simply went to sleep. He did not stay up all night worrying, fretting and rehearsing mentally the execution that awaited him in the morning. Rather he lay down with the chains, guards and steel bars and went to sleep. Peter didn't allow worry to weaken his faith. No matter what personal circumstances you face, the same victory awaits you, if you can keep your faith strong.

> Fret not thyself because of evil men, neither be thou envious at the wicked (Prov. 24:19).

> When the enemy shall come in like a flood, the Spirit of the Lord shall lift up a standard against him (Is. 59:19).

How simple this solution is: just go to sleep. Now how did this help preserve Simon Peter's strong faith? When you fall asleep, an end comes to the challenge that your hostile surroundings make to the promise of God. We have all spent sleepless nights rehearsing mentally the pending agonies of the coming morning. We would go to bed with strong faith, but, the longer we stayed awake, the more vivid the devil would make the possibilities of failure for the coming day. Those negative night scenes of failure weaken our faith; then fear and doubt begin to rule.

How much better off we would be if we would just fall asleep and keep our faith out of the reach of undue anxiety. When you are facing some great challenge in the coming morning, and it so troubles you that you cannot go to sleep, just get up. Turn the lights on. Open your Bible and read yourself back to sleep. Your faith won't deteriorate with Bible reading. If you just lie in the dark and let your imagination run wild, with scenes of horror of the coming day, it won't be long until your faith falters and weakens.

Simon Peter's faith was preserved by sleep. He simply closed out of his mind the negative night scenes that doubt and worry would bring by just going to sleep.

No door or chain that binds you can stand in a contest with your strong faith. Surely you can see from this illustration the pressing need to protect your faith from the attack of the devil, especially the attacks that come in the wee hours of the night, when you are tired and disoriented. So, whatever you do, don't just lie in bed rehearsing the worst scenarios of the coming morning. Go on to sleep. If you cannot go to sleep, get up and read your Bible until you fall asleep. Granted, this faith extender may not impress you as much as some of the others in the Bible. But, some time in the future, on the eve of a pending crisis, it may become the most important one in this book for you.

Whatever You Do, Don't Doubt God

For verily I say unto you, That whosoever shall say unto this mountain, Be thou removed, and be thou cast into the sea; and shall not doubt in his heart, but shall believe that those things which he saith shall come to pass, he shall have whatsoever he saith (Mark 11:23).

This powerful statement not only speaks of God's ability to control the circumstances that surround us, but it also clearly shows that we have a great part in accomplishing this process. We are told to speak forth those things we desire, without doubting. We do this so they can be given freely to us. This process works only if we speak in strong faith.

But let him ask in faith, nothing wavering [boldly, without doubt or hesitation]. For he that wavereth is like a wave of the sea driven with the wind and tossed. For let not that man think that he shall receive any thing of the Lord. A double minded man [the mind that thinks victory and failure

110

simultaneously] is unstable in all his ways (James
1:6-8).

These two verses are very special, because they awaken
us to the necessity of not just taking one verse and estab-
lishing a doctrine on it. Mark 11:23 speaks of the ability
we have to speak a thing and to have it come to pass.
However, our understanding of the verse in Mark will be
less than perfect until we add to it the clear teaching of
James 1:6-8. All of this speaking and asking must be in
the strongest of faith (nothing wavering) or it doesn't work.
This is why Paul said that he declared the whole counsel
of God to those He taught.

There are certain steps we must take to move the mountains, to change our circumstances or to manifest the
invisible. The process of producing God's best in our lives
is many times surrounded by adversity. In James 1:2, he
says to "count it all joy when you fall into various trials."

Songs and Praise Extend Faith

Paul and Silas employed faith extenders when they were
thrown into prison at Philippi. Instead of complaining, cry-
ing and having a pity party, they sang and praised God.
Neither Paul nor Silas was joyful over what had just happened to their physical bodies. Nor were they excited about
what was going to happen. But they were joyful over the
fact that their God was able to deliver them. There can
be no question about it; their faith was being tried.

In this trial, Paul and Silas could have murmured,
complained and licked their wounds. But they stood fast,
knowing that a double-minded man would not manifest
what they had need of in that hour. I say double-minded,
because it would be so easy for them to have been mind-
ful of the power of steel bars to hold them, instead of the

way of escape that God would provide. But they chose to be single of mind and only think thoughts of God's power to deliver. To accomplish this, they used an audible verbalization (words that could be heard) of songs. They rehearsed their God's love for them and His ability to change their undesirable circumstances.

You can also use audible verbalization. Audible verbalization is singing or speaking those things that you know God would want to happen to you. This is a very important way of controlling your circumstances. Your own voice speaking or singing God's desired result for you will strengthen your faith. It will make it easier for you to believe the things that God's Word says. You must learn how to say to the mountains of opposition, "Mountains, move out of the way." Speaking the removal of the undesirable is just as great a faith extender as speaking boldly the appearing of those things that you need.

Always keep this in mind: God does not want you to operate only in the natural realm. Here, in America, it is so very easy to have your material needs and desires met, especially if you have the motivation and skills to do so. Much of the time, in our nation, if you possess the drive and mental resources, it may seem faith is not needed to accomplish your secular or monetary goals. However, faith is just as needed in twentieth-century America as it is anywhere else, if we want to go beyond the natural realm. Now the natural is only temporary, while the spiritual is eternal.

> While we look not at the things which are seen, but at the things which are not seen: for the things which are seen are temporal; but the things which are not seen are eternal (2 Cor. 4:18).

Reach into the invisible realm for an eternal solution, if you need doors opened, or if you need deliverance from

112

things that hold you captive. Use the faith extenders of praise and worship to keep your faith strong, nothing wavering, and continuously receiving from God.

A New Testament Prophet Who Used Faith Extenders

The name of Agabus is not very familiar today. However, in the early New Testament days, his name was a household word. Agabus, the prophet, was the name by which he was known. The New Testament records an encounter between him and the great apostle Paul. In this encounter, Agabus used a very unique faith extender. The account of his prophecy to Paul and the faith extender is found in Acts.

> And the next day we that were of Paul's company departed, and came unto Caesarea: and we entered into the house of Philip the evangelist, which was one of the seven; and abode with him. And the same man had four daughters, virgins, which did prophesy. And as we tarried there many days, there came down from Judaea a certain prophet, named Agabus. And when he was come unto us, he took Paul's girdle, and bound his own hands and feet, and said, Thus saith the Holy Ghost, So shall the Jews at Jerusalem bind the man that owneth this girdle, and shall deliver him into the hands of the Gentiles. And when we heard these things, both we, and they of that place, besought him not to go up to Jerusalem (Acts 21:8-12).

Let me try to emphasize what took place, by paraphrasing what Agabus did. Agabus took Paul's girdle (probably a cloth that wrapped around his waist several times) and he bound up his own hands and feet with it. Hear him as he says, "Paul, do you see how I'm tied up? That is exactly

113

the way you are going to be tied up if you go to Jerusalem.'' Agabus portrayed vividly a picture of what the Holy Spirit had told him was going to happen.

Can't you just imagine the actions and words of Paul as he unwinds his girdle from Agabus's hands and feet and puts it back on himself? ''Thank you, dear friend, for the warning, but that is exactly what God wants to happen. I am to be bound by the Romans and shipped, as a common criminal, to Rome. There is a good reason for this, for I must tell Caesar and his court about Jesus.''

For many years, this account of Agabus and Paul was very hard for me to understand. One cannot read this portion of Scripture without asking some questions. What was the underlying problem here? Why the dramatics with Paul's waistband? Was Paul reluctant to hear the word of other prophets? Was Paul not to go? Was it necessary for this message to be given in the full company of everyone at the meeting? Wouldn't the contradiction to Paul's publicly stated plans be better given in private?

These questions plagued me for several years, until I was faced with giving a similar message to a great man of God to whom I was in submission. I had to speak contrary to the declared purpose of this senior minister of God. Even though God had spoken to me, I still found myself hard pressed to speak words of contradiction to this great man of God. I had to rephrase my words several times, as I found it increasingly difficult to deliver the Lord's message to this brother. It was very difficult to deliver uncompromisingly that which the Spirit of God had told me to say. I almost didn't do what God told me to do. To put it simply, I was intimidated by the awesome presence of this most anointed servant of God.

With this thought in mind, please allow me to present for your consideration an alternate explanation as to why Agabus bound his hands and feet with Paul's waistband.

I feel that Agabus had heard from God. Scripture proves that he knew what awaited Paul. However, Agabus's faith was wavering. Before you fault Agabus for this, remember Paul's stature. He was an apostle. Beyond this, Agabus was in submission to Paul.

Knowing Paul's determination, Agabus was under tremendous pressure. He had to stand publicly and prophesy that Paul's plan of going to Jerusalem would conclude with Paul being bound and imprisoned. But Agabus had seen all of this in the Spirit and he had to speak it. I believe when Agabus asked for Paul's waistband, and with it tied up his own hands and feet, he did not do it for the benefit of the great apostle. I believe he did it to strengthen his own wavering faith. This acting out of the fact that Paul's journey would end with his being bound and imprisoned made it impossible for Agabus to waiver when delivering that which the Holy Spirit had shown him. Once his hands and feet were bound with Paul's waistband, his prophecy had to come forth as he had heard from God.

How much surer I would have been, the time I was confronted with speaking to the senior minister, if I had used a simple faith extender as Agabus did. Surely it would have helped in keeping me from swerving from the exact message with which God had sent me.

Think about the things you might do that will help your faith remain strong, as you bring the message God gives you for others. Maybe you might say to a brother, "I have a message for you; when you have time, I will tell you." These words assure you that opportunity will arise. The normal curiosity of a human being will drive him to ask you what the message is. Simple faith extenders will help your faith not to wilt under the pressure of public witnessing or speaking a word from God. Just try it the next time you must face a person with a word from God or a word of correction.

When you want to give a person a gospel tract, you could just say, "I have something for you." When they say, "Now how about that thing you have for me," how much easier it will be to hand a tract to someone who asks for it. Try it; you'll like it.

We Are Not Adrift in the Stream of Life

Why all this teaching about strong faith? Why is it so important that you possess strong faith? Isn't the faith by which you were saved sufficient to live by? Your question may be, *Isn't everything about each life all planned ahead of time anyway? Aren't we just adrift on a predetermined stream of life, helplessly floating along to a predetermined destination?*

This form of thinking doesn't find its roots in God's Word. It developed when certain mistaken theologians came up with this conclusion—their own conclusion, I might add. They concluded that everything was predetermined and nothing was subject to change or correction. This destructive doctrinal position slowed evangelism and world missions for hundreds of years. It crippled the spiritual progress of generation after generation of saints. It kept the whole church from going on into perfection. This doctrine, called "hyper-Calvinism," has done much to impede the return of our Lord.

It is this erroneous doctrine which has caused many of God's children to be content with the lackluster state of mediocrity that constitutes nominal Christianity today. It has caused many Christians to drift aimlessly along the bottom of the stream of life. They never reach their God-ordained potential or even come close to approaching the good life God has awaiting them. This kind of theology shipwrecks the faith of multitudes who believe that God operates in the man-made concept of "absolute predestination." This irresponsible, noncommittal, low-achievement philosophy will never produce the proper climate or suitable soil for the growth of strong faith. Where this philosophy rules, there is no hope of possessing the victorious faith described by the apostle John—the kind of faith that "overcomes the world."

God has a plan for you that can, and will, change every negative circumstance in your life. You are not just adrift in the stream of life. God has a tailor-made plan for you that lies dormant, just beneath the surface of fear and doubt. It will arise out of dormancy with the kiss of strong faith.

Cast down the erroneous thinking of fatalism. You have been chosen to go from glory to glory into the image of Jesus. Your irrevocable ticket to that wondrous journey is your strong faith.

CHAPTER ELEVEN

Putting Faith Extenders To Work for You

It takes strong faith to walk confidently on planet earth as sons and daughters of God. God desires for us to walk as heirs of the promises that He made to our father, Abraham. If we ever plan to experience fully our inheritance, we must walk in the same strong faith as our father Abraham. As we attain this strong faith, we can easily tap into the great heavenly storehouses of God's abundant blessings.

However, before we can obtain God's best supply, we must learn to release old unscriptural notions, superstitions, traditions and negative attitudes. We must learn to stop struggling with new biblical concepts, even though they may challenge our traditional thinking patterns and doctrines. We must be willing to submit ourselves to change, not change that comes by the thoughts of men, but change that comes by the Word of God. If we can learn this, we will much more easily go from glory to glory into the marvelous image of our Lord and Savior, Jesus.

> But we all, with open face beholding as in a glass the glory of the Lord, are changed into the same image from glory to glory, even as by the Spirit of the Lord (2 Cor. 3:18).

Because of the influence of the shortage-mentality of the

world, the saints of God need constant reinforcement of the fact that we can possess all of the abundance God's Word says we can. I hope you do not still find yourself holding on to the mistaken notion that God does not want His children to be abundantly blessed. We discussed the fallacy of that kind of thinking in an earlier chapter. There we showed that the first miracle Jesus performed at Cana of Galilee was one of pure luxury—turning common water into the very finest of wine.

All of us have something we desire from God. We must begin today to speak our desire. We should not speak it with an attitude of hopelessness, but with great anticipation of receiving it. Make your request known to God, just as your own child would make it known to you. Go ahead, let your special, inward desire magnify and expand its existence by letting it be spoken from your mouth. Just speaking your desire out loud to God takes it one giant step closer to materialization. A spoken concept has much more substance than an unspoken concept.

The speaking of your desires causes them to acquire an added depth of substance. For instance, your desire might be peace of mind or the acquiring of knowledge. It doesn't matter what we desire to have. Whether it be health, a piano, the payment of unpaid bills, a new job, a godly wife or husband, a home, a car or a successful business, every desire must go through that first step of being spoken. This expands its substance from the realm of thoughts into the realm of a spoken concept. An unspoken thought or concept is without form until it is spoken. When it is spoken, it takes on form. It is actually increased in substance by three definite dimensions:

1. It can be seen. It can actually be seen and measured on an oscilloscope (a mechanism that displays the sound of words). It now vibrates in the conscious, tangible realm.

2. It can be heard. It takes on sound.

3. It takes up space wherever it goes. Everyone who hears it automatically gives space to it in their mind.

Two of the five senses can identify your desire's presence (hearing and seeing), whereas, before, your desire was without proof of its existence. Now it has multiple new dimensions. It is not only a thought or desire but has advanced to a spoken concept. When a desire is spoken, it receives added substance from God's Word, which says that whatever we say, not doubting, we shall have.

> And this is the confidence that we have in him, that, if we ask any thing according to his will, he heareth us (1 John 5:14).

God is not limited in His ability to supply. He says He will do more than we can ask or think (Eph. 3:20). As sons and daughters of the most high God we are heirs of His promised blessings.

Speak out that which you desire. God's own Son used this concept often. This concept of speaking our desires is a great faith extender. It will help our invisible desires to materialize more quickly in the visible realm. Speaking those things we desire is a biblical faith extender that we all should use. "Have faith in God," for you "shall have whatsoever" you say (Mark 11:22,23).

You should operate faith extenders in your life. So let's learn how to make faith extenders work for us in our everyday lives. There is great potential in faith extenders to expand the faith of all the saints of God, enabling them to enjoy all the benefits of sonship.

A Proper Self-Image—
A Prerequisite to Possessing the Promise

Without a proper biblical self-image, you will not be able to cultivate the strong faith necessary to possess the portion God has set aside for you.

> Behold that which I have seen: it is good and comely
> for one to eat and to drink, and to enjoy the good
> of all his labor that he taketh under the sun all the
> days of his life, which God giveth him: for it is his
> portion (Eccl. 5:18).

Faith stays shallow and weak if you have a mental self-image that is less than the dynamic image that the Word of God gives of you.

You must cast down the evil imaginations of yourself as a weakling. The Bible says to renew your mind and fill it with a proper self-image, seeing yourself as the Bible describes you—an overcomer right now—not some day in the "sweet by and by," but right now. You must fully believe and boldly proclaim that you are the righteousness of God in Christ Jesus.

> But now the righteousness of God without the law
> is manifested, being witnessed by the law and the
> prophets; even the righteousness of God which is
> by faith of Jesus Christ unto all and upon all them
> that believe (Rom. 3:21,22).

You have the divinely given right to proclaim that you are the righteousness of God in Christ.

> For he hath made him to be sin for us, who knew
> no sin; that we might be made the righteousness of
> God in him (2 Cor. 5:21).

Do not minimize this faith extender. For without a proper biblical self-image, you will be open to daily setbacks and defeats from Satan. He will make quick work of any saint suffering from an identity crisis (not knowing who they are in Christ).

Every time your spirit, soul and body hear you declare

who you are in Christ, you (spirit, soul and body) grow stronger. Always give yourself every advantage in your warfare with Satan. Speak clearly, concisely and boldly of who you really are in Christ. Don't speak words of life into your old fallen nature by referring to yourself as a weakling, a sinner, a worm or one who is indecisive, as though you still had to live in that defeated state. You are a new creature (species); old things have passed away...all things are become new (2 Cor. 5:17). Do yourself and your God the courtesy of speaking of yourself in the same way and with the same honor that the Bible does.

An identity crisis is among the worst crises in which anyone can find themselves. When you do not clearly know who you are, it will be impossible to approach your enemy properly and overcome him. It will also be impossible to approach your God and move into proper relationship with Him to rule and reign.

Let me give you an illustration of the peril of an identity crisis. If a person contracts amnesia, he loses the use of all of the blessings and privileges he has as a human being. While his memory is lost, his assets are not at his disposal. His precious feelings of relationships are lost to him. His influence is not at his disposal. If, however, he regains his knowledge of who he is, all these blessings and privileges would once again be at his disposal. He would not be poor. He would not be without relationships, nor would he be without influence. If you do not know who you are in Christ, you cannot walk in the full benefit of your privileges and supply.

Breaking the Defeatist Attitude

At one time or another, everyone has the feeling of being inadequate or defeated. Perhaps, even at this time, you are experiencing these feelings. Maybe you still believe something negative that your parents, friends or peers told you about yourself. Let me give you an example. You may have grown up in a very negative environment. Those around you may have continually told you that you are no good, you will never amount to anything or you're dumb! Many of these negative comments produce wrong mental attitudes—attitudes that go directly against what God says you are. These thoughtless descriptions of you will, many times, come to haunt you as an adult. Most negative feelings can be traced back to childhood suggestions that some unthinking or insecure person systematically loaded into our thought patterns.

If Jesus is who He says He is, and if He amounts to anything at all in this universe, you, as His brother or His sister (bone of His bone and flesh of His flesh), must, without question, also amount to something.

> For we which live are alway delivered unto death for Jesus' sake, that the life also of Jesus might be made manifest in our mortal flesh (2 Cor. 4:11).

The Bible states that you are becoming everything that Jesus is. When you were born again, you began a metamorphosis (a changing of your being) from glory to glory into Christ's marvelous image.

> But we all, with unveiled face, beholding as in a mirror the glory of the Lord, are being transformed in the same image [the image of His glory] from glory to glory, just as by the Spirit of the Lord (2 Cor. 3:18, NKJV).

You are, right now, the righteousness of God, because of His abundant and effective grace. A bad mental image of yourself will lessen your productivity and value to God and His kingdom. You will be as the proverbial fruitless fig tree, which Jesus cursed and smote.

124

Begin today to get rid of that terrible weight of a poor self-image. A poor self-image is unscriptural, as well as devastating to your success as a maturing, accumulating, overcoming saint of God. When I say accumulating, I speak of the accumulation of spiritual as well as physical possessions—possessions that are ours for the taking, if we have faith to believe that we can receive every promise to us in the Bible.

You Can Do God's Will

When you can't seem to overcome even the simplest habit, usually a good faith extender can help! The inability to overcome a bad habit usually happens to Christians because the stronghold of that habit is either consciously or subconsciously being reinforced. One exceptionally devastating way you can reinforce a bad habit's power over you is by speaking that you cannot quit that habit. Don't you see that each time you say you can't quit, you increase the habit's hold on you. You might say that this type of a confession is a negative faith extender that weakens faith. Doesn't it just stand to reason that a good positive confession such as "I can quit" or "I have quit" will greatly weaken the power of the habit and measurably strengthen your ability to overcome it? If you do this convincingly and consistently, it will surely lead to the breaking of the habit. Every time you say you cannot do that which God wants you to do, you guarantee your continuing failure in that area.

Poverty a Possible Addiction

Not all addictions are the obvious kinds, such as smoking, drinking or narcotics. Some are much less obvious, but no less addictive. Let's look at a less obvious

125

addiction—poverty. Some folks just cannot break loose of its awful grip. The reason for this is that they have bound themselves to the spirit or mentality of poverty. They do this by saying it is impossible for them to exist in any other financial state. These people also allow no other mental picture of themselves than that of seeing themselves endlessly existing in poverty. Therefore, just as surely as they allow no other mental picture of themselves than being in poverty, they tie themselves inseparably to poverty.

Bad Health a Possible Addiction

One of the most insidious habits known to man is the habit of bad health. I know that some people are really sick. But many are in the habit of being sick. It has been estimated that well over half of the world's sick suffer from an illness that is psychosomatic (imagined sickness). They are causing themselves to be bound needlessly to ill health. Faithless words from their own mouths and continuous anticipation of contracting whatever might be going around at the time keeps them on a collision course with sickness. How very binding are the fetters that negative words and negative anticipations form.

God wants to break those bondages. I want you to mark these next words. The word "can't," when spoken by Christians in reference to God's will for their lives, is not proper grammar. Hear God's Word and live. It says that the children of God can do (not can't do) all things through Jesus Christ who strengthens them (notice, strengthens—increases their faith).

I can do all things through Christ which strengtheneth me (Phil. 4:13).

You might be asking, "Do you really believe you can do all things through Christ?" My natural mind (the logical

126

mind) does not know how this would be possible. But I am not just a natural man. I am a spirit man. I must believe that which the Scriptures say. I must "let" the mind of Christ be in me. If I let the mind of Christ be in me, it will bring every thought into obedience to the knowledge of God (2 Cor. 10:5). If I uncompromisingly accept that the superior witness of Christ is true, I must then reject the inferior witness of my carnal mind and my natural circumstances. With His mind, I can, without flinching, accept and believe that I can do all things through Christ who strengthens me—and so can you!

How mightily this process works. While my natural mind is saying, "No, you can't do the things God requires!," my spiritual mind is saying, "Yes, I can do all things!" Think with me of the amplifying effect that a powerful confession has on our faith. You see, I have the ability, in any situation, to make one of my thoughts more real than the other.

If I say, "I can't," with my words I fortify and intensify my inabilities. If I say, "I can do all things through Christ who strengthens me," I fortify and intensify my ability.

I am well aware that just saying, "I can," doesn't make a thing happen. It does, however, bring it one step closer to happening. By speaking enabling thoughts and refusing to speak negative, disabling thoughts, I strengthen the possibility that what I would do will come to pass. I give the spoken thought the superior dimension of being not only a thought, but also a spoken concept—a concept which then lives not only in my mind but which can enter the minds of others.

Remember to speak with your mouth what the mind of Christ within you is saying is possible. With this, measurable amounts of energy are released into the atmosphere— energy that will bring pressure to bear on your adverse circumstances. This pressure will influence them to come into line with the will of God for your life. Words are among the greatest faith extenders in the Bible.

Beat your plowshares into swords, and your pruninghooks into spears: Let the weak say, I am strong (Joel 3:10).

(As it is written, I have made thee a father of many nations,) before him whom he believed, even God, who quickeneth the dead, and calleth those things which be not as though they were (Rom. 4:17).

And this is the confidence that we have in him, that, if we ask any thing according to his will, he heareth us (1 John 5:14).

A Beginning Point—Speaking the Desire

To start, take an initial step by beginning to speak the things you desire boldly, graphically and as if they already existed. Now remember, there is nothing dishonest in doing this. They may not exist in totally manifested, material form, but when you speak them in faith, believing, they do exist in a pre-materialized form.

God's Word says that there are several pre-materialization dimensions—dimensions where the things we desire or need exist before they are manifested.

1. The things God says will come to pass.

For verily I say unto you, Till heaven and earth pass, not one jot or one tittle shall in no wise pass from the law, till all be fulfilled (Matt. 5:18).

2. The things we hope for.

Now faith is the substance of things hoped for (Heb. 11:1).

3. The yet unmanifested things we speak will exist.

> Whosoever...shall not doubt in his heart, but shall believe that those things which he saith shall come to pass; he shall have whatsoever he saith (Mark 11:23).

This is how God operates, speaking those things that are not as if they were.

> God, who...calleth those things which be not as though they were (Rom. 4:17).

Illustrations of Faith Extenders

Let's use an illustration of the principle of speaking your desire. Say that you desire to go somewhere special—perhaps Hawaii, the Holy Land or some special Bible conference. For illustration purposes, let's say it's Hawaii. To begin with, start saying, "I am going to Hawaii!" You may not have the money to go at this time, but don't allow that as-yet-unresolved circumstance to stop you. Allow your desire to progress from its dimensionally nebulous state (almost without definable dimensions) of a mere desire into the superior multi-dimensional state (that which has several discernable dimensions) of a spoken concept. Notice carefully how I have worded your desire not as a mere wish, but as a sure thing. Not "*I want* to go to Hawaii," but "*I am going* to Hawaii." With these words, your desire has progressed beyond the uncertain status of a wish or whim to the substantive status of an attested coming event.

In this positive form, anticipation can begin to fortify and enhance the concept, drawing it ever closer to fulfillment. Don't keep this good news to yourself. Daily tell your friends that your Hawaii trip is certain. Do not become frustrated if you are asked when you are going. Just tell them that you are working out the details. Do you see? The issue now is not if you are going, but when you are going. Notice how you have upgraded the quality of this desire by stating it positively as a fact, instead of a mere whim.

Perhaps your great desire is to give $1,000 during the next twelve months to a ministry (your church or its building fund, an evangelist, Christian television, and so forth). Say the thing that you desire: "I am going to give $1,000 this year to ____" (insert the name of the ministry).

To take this beyond the mere status of a wish, take some definite steps toward fulfilling that desire.

Start with first speaking out loud, "I am going to give $1,000 to my favorite ministry."

Second, divide the $1,000 by the twelve months in a year. This brings the monthly amount you must give to $83.33. All of a sudden it seems much more feasible, but still pretty high for most folks.

Next, divide the $1,000 by the fifty-two weeks in a year. This would bring the amount you would have to give each week to $19.25. That's less than $20 per week. It doesn't seem nearly so overwhelming as $1,000 seemed.

Then call or write to your favorite ministry and ask them to agree with you that you will, by faith, give $1,000 either by the week or by the month.

Notice the progression:

1. The $1,000 was a mere thought.

2. It became a spoken concept.

3. It took on new dimensions when you wrote it down and explored the mathematical possibilities of paying it by the month or by the week.

4. Your desire was shared with the recipient, and he or she came into agreement with you.

Every step was an expansion of the desire that brought

it closer to reality.

The faith extenders of positive confession begin to work for you after you take the first step of speaking that which God has put in your heart. Then other faith extenders follow as you implement as much of the plan as possible. My dictionary says that implementing means to give practical effect, to ensure actual fulfillment. The more implementing you do, along with a positive confession, the more assured you are of the manifestation of your desires.

Of course, it goes without saying that this must be accompanied by earnest prayer and diligent work.

> Faith, if it hath not works, is dead, being alone (James 2:17).

CHAPTER TWELVE

Faith Extenders
That Can Help You

My oldest daughter, Martina Yvette, is the secretary for my ministry. She and her two children, Martina and Johnny, lived for a period of time in a home the ministry provided. One day she decided it was time she owned a home of her own. She had no down payment and no substantial credit. In the natural, it seemed like owning a home was an impossibility.

But in faith she called a real estate agent. She gave him a description of the house, the number of rooms, the desired living area and the part of the city in which it had to be located. One very important item she requested was that the house would require no down payment. If she had not become specific and put her faith to work by engaging a real estate agent, they would still be in the home the ministry provided. But when she declared it and put her faith to work, she soon had the house. It was right there waiting for her. But it would never have become a reality in her life if she had not had the kind of faith that went to work.

You may have a dream house. It might be sitting there right now, occupied by owners who are just waiting for your call. It might be vacant and belong to a builder who is super-motivated to sell it at your price and terms. The faith extender my daughter used was to contact the realtor and get the search started for that which only existed in her imagination.

Breaking the Cycle of Insufficiency

The process of speaking those things that are not as if they were works in many realms. Perhaps you are poor, hungry and destitute. Think about it. What possible strength can you draw on by saying, "Yesterday I was poor, hungry and destitute, and tomorrow will probably be worse." It depresses me just to write such a statement. Don't you see that this kind of affirmation of the negative forces now dominating your circumstances does nothing more than fortify and strengthen that undesirable situation? The very situation that you so desperately want to change is fortified by your words. Negative statements about your insufficiency will only strengthen the grip of insufficiency on your life.

Throughout His Word, God is trying to teach you to walk by faith. Actually, He is trying to get you to put off the old man who walks in his circumstances. He wants you to walk in what I like to call the "new creation man" (see 2 Cor. 5:17; Gal. 6:15,16). The new creation man is an overcomer and walks in God's perfect will. He doesn't go around bellyaching about his problems and declaring their power over him. He is continuously challenging and rising above that which attempts to keep him from God's best.

The new creation man flatly rejects that which the curse from the Garden of Eden has brought upon him. He proclaims the blessings that Christ has purchased for him. He speaks those things that are not yet manifested as if they already were. It is only right that the new creation man does this, because he knows that he is a partaker of the divine nature of God—the new nature every Christian

134

eceives from God and is clearly spoken of in Scripture.

Whereby are given unto us exceeding great and precious promises: that by these ye might be partakers of the divine nature (2 Pet. 1:4).

If you are God's child, then He desires you to act like Him. He wants you to have His divine nature. In situations that are less than what He desires them to be, God peaks of them as He wills them to be. He boldly declares uture events to be as He wants them. He never confesses ack, because He is the God of abundance. Wherever He ules, abundance is present. When His Son appeared in srael during the time of Roman dominion, poverty and hortage were everywhere. But Jesus did not go about leclaring insufficiency. He declared that, with His arrival, here also arrived great abundance.

I am come that they might have life...more abundantly (John 10:10).

Living Faith Is Doing Faith

Even so faith, if it hath not works, is dead, being alone (James 2:17).

Strong faith is faith which engages actively in works. The apostle James makes short work of the erroneous impression that faith waits on God to do the work. You see, God isn't looking for someone to work for. God is looking for someone to work with and in.

They went...every where, the Lord working with them, and confirming the word with signs following (Mark 16:20).

Living faith is working faith. Here is an example of this principle:

Perhaps God has impressed you to write a book. Begin by saying that you are going to write a book. Don't just say this, but add faith to your statement—the kind of faith that James described—the kind that works. Get some paper and start writing down the thoughts God gives you. Research your topic. Think of a title. Use the faith extender of visualization and see yourself writing a book.

Recognize how powerful the faith extender of visualization would be at this point. The mental picture of yourself writing a book fortifies the confession you are making that you will write a book. Each step gives more substance to that which only a short time before had been only an impression of God in your spirit.

I do this with each book I write. I state that I am in the process of writing each book that God gives me an idea for, no matter what stage of development it is in. This very book, *Faith Extenders*, has had the status of being called a book for almost ten years before it went to press. Six other books have been written and published since I began this book. It was first targeted to be a twenty-four-page booklet, but, as you see, it has developed well beyond that. For many years it floundered, seemingly going nowhere. Yet I have always referred to this book as a book I *am* writing—one of the several that I *am* always writing.

Another faith extender I use with each book I write is that as soon as I have a subject and a title, I state, both publicly and in my inner thoughts, that the book is at least twenty-five percent completed. I also might mention here that about half of the time God changes the title of the book before it goes to press. For instance, my fifth book, *Financing the Endtime Harvest—God's Way*, went all the way up to the typesetting stage with another name before God changed the title. Up until that time, it had been entitled *90 Lessons in the Principles of Biblical Economics*.

Always be ready to hear God. Hearing God takes many

forms. In the case of the book *Financing the Endtime Harvest—God's Way*, God spoke to me through a man I respect very much. I asked Paul Crouch of Trinity Broadcasting Network to read the manuscript and comment on it, and he was very moved. He was moved, that is, with everything except the title. He commented that the title didn't seem to be God's best. Well, as I checked with God, He gave me a title far superior to the one I had chosen. Always be open to the many ways God can speak to you.

Maybe your calling is not to be a writer. Maybe you are called of God to be a gospel singer. Please keep in mind that if God has called you to sing, He will give you talent in singing. Now this doesn't mean that everyone will immediately say you are a good singer. But, probably, someone who has an ear for music will confirm that you have a good voice. You may say, "But I don't have a place to sing." Yes, you do! Start singing in the bathtub. Give your first "concerts" in the privacy of your shower.

See yourself, in your imagination, singing before an audience. Look for a church that needs the ministry of a singer. Tell the pastors of the churches in your area that you are available to sing. You may want to have some simple business cards available. Attend community gospel sings and give the person in charge a copy of your business card.

In short, let your faith be the kind that is alive and at work. Get plenty of faith extenders involved. They will help to keep you from becoming discouraged. They will help you to keep driving toward the fulfillment of your God-given goal. Your strong faith—faith that has been amplified by some good faith extenders—is a necessary part of materializing your career. Remember these two verses:

FAITH EXTENDERS

Faith is the substance of things hoped for, the evidence of things not seen (Heb. 11:1).

For as the body without the spirit is dead, so faith without works is dead also (James 2:26).

CHAPTER THIRTEEN

Faith Extenders
Used in Healing

Is any sick among you? Let him call for the elders
of the church; and let them pray over him, anointing him with oil in the name of the Lord: And the
prayer of faith shall save the sick, and the Lord shall
raise him up; and if he have committed sins, they
shall be forgiven him (James 5:14,15).

Please examine these biblical instructions closely. What
information is the apostle desiring to convey to us? The
first thing he says is, "*Is* there any sick among you?"
Notice the faith extender in the way he states the question. He doesn't presuppose that some would be sick by
saying, "The sick among you should call the elders." That
would fortify the power of sickness. Instead, he speaks
to them as those who have strong enough faith that there
would be no sick among them. If, however, there were
ever any sick ones among them, let them call for the elders.

The question comes to mind: Why should the sick call
for the elders? Surely the apostle knew that they could go
directly to Jesus with their illnesses. The reason for this
is that the elders would be like a faith extender to the
weaker saints—those who, because of weakened faith, need
help in reaching out beyond the circumstances of sickness.
Those with weak faith cannot seem to lay hold of the

healing that is already theirs.

> By whose stripes ye *were* healed (1 Pet. 2:24, italics mine).

All the divine healing of the saints is already accomplished and has been accomplished, since the moment the last stripe by the cruel cat-o'-nine-tails was laid on the back of Jesus. The apostle James tells us to call the elders to let them act out (faith extender) healing for the sick saint. He tells them to bring the oil and role-play the healing for them. He tells today's elders to present an illustrated sermon of the healing that Christ purchased for all of us some 2,000 years ago.

When called by the sick person, elders stand in as a type of the sick saint's elder brother Jesus. So, as we call the elders, they will role-play the healing work of Jesus through the operation of the Holy Spirit. The oil, which is applied to the body of the sick person by the elders, is traditionally believed to be a type of the Holy Spirit. As the elder applies the oil to the sick person's body, he or she can more easily visualize the healing flow from God through the ministry of the Holy Spirit. This visualization makes that which happened years ago at a cruel Roman whipping post come to life and find its fulfillment in meeting the sick person's need. The elders' physical presence, plus the symbolic presence of the Holy Ghost (the oil), reinforces and joins with the faith of the sick saint, making it easier for him to lay hold on God's promise of healing.

> And with his stripes, we *are* healed (Is. 53:5, italics mine).

The elders' anointing with oil becomes a faith extender. Their presence helps to strengthen weakened faith. It gives a symbolic substance to the invisible realm from which healing emanates. The whole process of calling the elders to anoint with oil is for those with weak faith, as a faith extender, or amplifier, to reinforce and extend faith.

Every time the elders anoint with oil, a powerful visualization process takes place. For almost 2,000 years, the church of Jesus Christ has had at its disposal this great faith extender, given by the apostle James. How wonderfully our God provides these helpers for our faith, causing us to be able to reach far beyond ourselves and lay hold upon God's provision. Faith extenders can amplify sub-mustard-seed-sized faith into mountain-moving faith— faith that can quickly overcome and evict from our bodies any sickness that has taken up residence.

You Have Used Faith Extenders

Think of the times you have heard a preacher encourage you to hold your hands out in a cup-like fashion when you were praying for your healing. He was asking you to make a faith-extending gesture so you might more easily receive that which the Holy Spirit willingly wants to pour out upon you.

A simple gesture, like cupping your hands, as you ask God in prayer to heal you, is a faith extender. It is something which makes it a bit easier for our minds to take hold of something in the invisible realm (our healing). When we are full of anticipation, it is easier to take hold of the readily available blessings of God. A simple faith extender can amplify our faith, allowing us to possess God's promised supply.

I have seen the use of this simple faith extender (the cupped hands uplifted to God) transform seemingly uneventful song services into a healing revival, as the song leader would, upon singing the song, "Fill My Cup, Lord," ask the congregation to cup their hands and hold them up to God. He would then have the instruments stop playing as the people sang a cappella and focused their attention on receiving from God. Then the now-extended faith and heightened anticipation of receiving suddenly ignited the imagination of the believers with a consciousness of the presence of God, and immediately many miracles were released.

People often pray for the healing power of God to minister to their physical need through just such a faith intensifier as this, and, with the help of such a simple gesture, are catapulted into a higher spiritual realm—a realm just above doubt, where the receiving of the blessings of God happens freely.

Faith extenders, while little understood and greatly underestimated, have consistently, throughout the history of the church, been used to fan the sparks of weak faith into hot, strong faith.

When we pray for a healing, it is very important that the person praying believes their miracle healing will be accomplished without doubt. Unwavering trust in the ability of our miracle-working God is of the utmost importance for healing to take effect. While we know that the Scriptures declare all can be healed, each praying individual must still believe it. We must be able to reach, by faith, beyond the natural realm of sickness into the supernatural realm of the desired healing.

Each of us should thank God for any faith extender that lifts us above our impossibilities into the realm of God's possibilities.

I have witnessed many marvelous faith healings and have received several wonderful healings myself. I have also been used of God, upon many occasions, to administer faith healing. The methods of administering faith healing vary from person to person. God said there would be varied administrations of the gifts (1 Cor. 12:5). Some will lay hands on the sick person. Some will anoint with oil. Some will speak to God. Some will speak to the sickness. Some will encourage the recipients to raise their hands or cup them. Others will encourage the recital of a prayer. Still others will have the sick person rebuke the illness.

These varying ways of administering healing are all forms of faith extenders and are designed to accomplish the same desired results—building faith strong enough to lay hold of that which God has promised. Keep in mind that the healing itself was accomplished 2,000 years ago. Now it simply awaits appropriation through strong faith.

Let me clarify. I have just lumped into one group several things you probably would not have categorized as faith extenders—laying on of hands, anointing with oil, speaking to sicknesses, and so forth. While all of these have a very strong basis in Scripture, and each helps to effect the healing process, the saints of God must remember that healing by faith does not find its source in these processes. Faith healing finds its source in the stripes that were placed on the back of Jesus. When our eyes are opened to faith extenders, it is easy to see that these God-ordained activities tend to intensify our faith. Please keep in mind that my comments about these activities are not all-inclusive but general in their scope.

Is It Wrong to Deny Sickness?

Is it right to say you are not sick, when, in fact, you have every symptom of a sickness? This is a legitimate question.

How often do we witness the following scenario: A saint of God is going about sniffling and coughing and is asked, "Are you sick?"

He answers in a rough, cough-racked voice, "Oh, no, I'm just fine." Cough, cough, sniffle.

Unwittingly, the questioning person might press him a bit by saying, "Are you sure you're not sick? You sound and look as if you are sick."

Steadfastly the saint replies, with all the confidence that he can muster amidst the coughing and multiple sneezes, "I am just fine. By His stripes, I am healed!"

With one last effort at reconciling the contradiction that the questioner is witnessing, he might dare just one more time to say, "Well, you look sick to me."

Then, stubbornly, with great resolve, the afflicted saint will reply, "You can't believe everything you see."

This is an example of a conversation between one who knows what the Word says about healing and a person who has no knowledge of the Bible fact that "with His stripes we *are* healed." The afflicted saint knows the sickness exists and that it has taken up residence in his body. He, more than anyone, knows that. He believes that what God says supercedes what the symptoms say.

He knows that his body and mind will be greatly influenced by what he says about the invading sickness. If he confesses that the sickness has overtaken his immune system, he tends to give strength to the sickness. He knows that this kind of confession speaks weakness to his immune system. And, besides all this, the Bible says the sickness has no right to be in his body in the first place. Any words of acknowledgement of the sickness would subconsciously tend to fortify the sickness's hold on his body. Acknowledging the sickness would also tend to weaken faith—faith that is at that very moment attempting to reach into the Spirit world and manifest the healing that has already been purchased for him.

When Christians deny sickness, they are simply saying that they believe Isaiah 53:5 more than they believe the symptoms of their sickness.

You see, almost 2,000 years ago, Jesus' back was

covered with the stripes from a rough Roman scourge. By His suffering of those cruel stripes, the Word of God says that everyone who has been saved has also been healed. There are two verses that sound much alike; they are very important in the fact of healing. The first one is in Isaiah 53:5, which says that with His stripes, we *are* healed (speaking of ability). The second one is 1 Peter 2:24, which says that by His stripes we *were* healed (speaking of accomplishment). Since the death of Jesus on the cross, the status of Isaiah 53:5 has been upgraded from an available remedy to the better status of an accomplished cure.

How quickly uninformed people tend to become impatient with the child of God who is bold enough to speak out a faith-extending confession—a confession that speaks the truth of the Word of God over and above the manifestations of a sickness. For the uninformed, it is hard to understand that this person isn't lying. He or she has chosen to confess the greater truth. They choose to say that which God says about their body's health over and above what Satan is trying to manifest in it. The Bible says that 2,000 years ago every saint was healed by the stripes that were laid on our precious Savior's back.

You should definitely not be discouraged or embarrassed as you reach out in your strongest possible faith to lay hold of the healing that Jesus purchased for you. *Under no circumstances* should you ever despair and allow yourself to give up on actively seeking your healing. Seek your healing by all means possible. Especially seek your healing through strong faith. By all means, you must keep on standing firm in the knowledge of your healing. You must keep on confessing faithfully God's solution to your health problem (the stripes of Jesus).

Confessing the yet unmanifested is exactly what God does. We understand from 2 Peter 1:4 that we are "partakers of His divine nature." In 2 Corinthians 3:18 we read that we're being changed from glory to glory into His marvelous image. The Scriptures reveal that we are becoming like Him. Let's help the process. Let's start to speak as He speaks. Make the confession of your faith positive and in direct line with God's Word. Don't let it be in line with your circumstances, problems or symptoms.

Rebuke Not a Brother

As you now begin to walk in the truth that you have learned about the positive confession, remember that the positive confession is a faith extender that God has given to us for our individual use. We should never correct someone else harshly in the body of Christ, if he or she is not mature enough to operate in the principle of the positive confession. The positive confession is designed for the person with advanced biblical knowledge.

You might walk up to another Christian who is coughing and sneezing and ask him, ''Are you sick?''

If he says, ''Yes,'' don't start telling him, in a harsh way, that this is a bad confession and he will stay sick as long as he confesses the sickness. First of all, ask to pray for him. Remember, some who had no faith of their own were healed by the strong faith of others.

And when they could not come nigh unto him for the press, they uncovered the roof where he was: and when they had broken it up, they let down the bed wherein the sick of the palsy lay. When Jesus saw their faith, he said unto the sick of the palsy, Son, thy sins be forgiven thee (Mark 2:4, 5).

When the sneezing saint knows of your concern for his situation, you can share with him the truth you know about the positive confession as a faith extender. He may not know that his words are powerful enough to influence his situation. Whatever you do, however, don't put condemnation upon him with harsh rebukes. Treat him as our Lord would have treated him—with love.

Strong Faith Has a Profound Effect on Your Health

Use your imagination to see things the way God intends them to be, instead of as they are. To do this, you will need a good, concise mental picture of God's will for your future. If you are not enjoying good health, project pictures of yourself in the best of health on the screen of your imagination.

This process worked for me. A number of years ago, I fell from a considerable height, fracturing a vertebra in my back and breaking both of my feet. My left foot was badly broken and mended so poorly that I could not walk without great pain and a noticeable limp. The doctors said I would have a severe limp for the rest of my life. They also said I would have absolutely no side motion in my left foot.

I was not ready to accept that prognosis. I practiced a form of faith extension religiously. I refused to refer to myself as one who limped, even though my limp was very severe. And further, I imagined myself walking perfectly, without even the slightest limp. I constantly (in my imagination) visualized myself whole and walking normally. I forced myself to be conscious of the sound my feet made as I walked. I listened closely to the sound my feet made as they struck the pavement and relentlessly worked at getting my crippled foot to sound exactly like the good one. As I took each step, I kept a mental picture of myself walking effortlessly and flawlessly without a limp.

The medical proof of the working of these faith extenders came to me one day as I visited my father's home in Florida. My father has a friend who is one of the foremost bone surgeons in the world. He is one of a team of men who pioneered the development of the mechanical hip socket. After thoroughly checking my feet by X-rays, he said, "You have had the worst kind of break possible on your left foot. People who suffer from that kind of break always lose their ability to move their foot from side to side."

When he asked me if this was the case with my foot, I showed him the almost full range of movement I now have in my foot. He was surprised that I had recovered such a great range of side movement in my foot. His next question to me was, "How did you accomplish that?"

I said, "At night when I go to bed, I pull the bed covers down real tight over my foot causing it to be forced to the right, like this (I showed him). The following night, I reverse the process and pull the bed covers down extra tight with my foot forced the other way" (I showed him again). Each night I forced my foot to turn as far as possible in the direction that the break had robbed me of movement. I caused the covers to hold it in the position that every doctor had said it would never again go into of its own power. I refused to accept the fact that side-to-side motion would be robbed from that foot.

The bone doctor thought my healing and the recovery of side movement to my left foot were remarkable.

He said that in his examination he had found that my left leg was now shorter than the other. He said, "Now let me see you walk. I want to observe the severity of your limp."

I walked across the room and after observing me in amazement, he said, "My goodness, you don't limp at all!" His next question was, "Can you also walk on an uneven or sloped terrain without feeling pain?"

"Yes," I said. Again he was amazed.

He told me of treating a man whose occupation was

roofing. It seems that this roofer had a break in his foot in exactly the same place and manner as mine. The only difference was that the man could no longer walk on a slanted surface, such as a roof. This caused him to lose his job in the roofing trade.

"I can walk on slanted roofs," I replied. "When I do it for a long period, it does hurt a bit, but not enough to deter me."

This has been a very significant faith extender for me, as today I travel worldwide, walking through airports, constantly carrying heavy baggage.

I am totally healed of that terrible accident as a result of two things: the stripes of Jesus and good faith extenders.

The "break" and the limping were Satan's will for my foot, but walking without a limp is God's will. I chose to choose God's will for my life. I believe that I can achieve that which His Word says. What Satan means for evil in our lives, God will turn into good for those who have strong faith.

You have a choice as to which pictures you run in your imagination. Remember, "as he thinketh in his heart, so is he" (Prov. 23:7).

CHAPTER FOURTEEN

The World Unwittingly Uses Faith Extenders

Worldly advertising agencies openly, and without excuse, use the principles of God's faith extenders.

Suppose you go to the store to buy toothpaste. Immediately, bewilderment will set in, as you are faced with the gigantic section marked "toothpaste." Your mind asks, "Which one should I buy?" Quickly, your memory banks respond with a catchy little tune and the words of a familiar television jingle which accompanies some particular toothpaste commercial. As your mind rehearses the words of the jingle, the name of the toothpaste in the jingle corresponds with the brand that has the largest advertising budget. Instead of leaving your mind clear to choose a brand based on some more meritorious reason, a jingle chooses for you.

Commercial slogans and songs are like miniature memory enhancers or amplifiers which consciously, as well as subconsciously, influence a future purchasing decision.

An illustration of the power of toothpaste jingles can be seen from my own experience. When I was writing this portion of the book (in one of its first drafts), I illustrated the power of a jingle by saying that when I came to the toothpaste section of the store, I always heard a familiar jingle go off in my mind. It went like this, "Brusha',

brusha', brusha'—new Ipana toothpaste.'' My mind always goes to Ipana toothpaste. I don't use Ipana. In fact, I have never used Ipana; but their jingle is locked into my thought process.

Here is the significance of this illustration. When I was having the handwritten manuscript of this book typed, the young lady (about ten to fifteen years younger than myself) said she had never heard a jingle with these words. I realized that I had heard that jingle over thirty years before—not on television, but on the radio, as a young boy. It had stayed in my mind all that time and, even today, forty years later, it dominates my thoughts when toothpaste is mentioned.

In Selling Paint

The paint industry uses the principles of faith extenders. When you enter a paint store to buy paint, you usually pass a table with little, paddle-shaped wooden sticks on it. These are ideal for stirring paint, and yes, you guessed it, they are free. ''Please take several,'' the sign says. On the stick is the brand name of a popular paint manufacturer. This is a built-in memory stimulator. The manufacturer is not concerned that you have a nice paint paddle. He is, however, concerned that you purchase his paint. With that paddle, he has put you ever so slightly in his debt, for now you are walking about the store with a gift he gave you.

There is an Old Testament concept of advertising which the Madison Avenue executives would like the world to believe originated with them, but God was the first one to use this principle. God used memory enhancement in the Old Testament, when He commanded the children of Israel to bind the Scriptures upon their foreheads. There, in open view, on their foreheads, the Scriptures were always visible to every Israelite they met. As they greeted each other, each time their eyes met, the Word of God would be just a fraction of an inch above the eyes of the person at whom they were looking. This ingenious faith extender reminded all of Israel that they were the chosen people of God, with a written word from their God.

With this in mind, let's continue our visit in the paint store. If you're going to do some painting, you need a painter's cap. No one ever buys a painter's cap; they are not for sale. The paint company insists on giving you one free, and, sure enough, there it is, the name of the paint manufacturer printed boldly across the front and the back of the cap. Everyone in the store is getting into the spirit of painting. Rather than carrying the caps in their hands, they are putting on the free paint caps. When they look at each other's faces, the prominent thing they see is the paint manufacturer's name written across each other's caps.

Haven't we heard of forehead advertising somewhere before? If the world has learned to use faith-extending principles of God, shouldn't we, the children of God, use them? No wonder Jesus said, "The children of this world are in their generation wiser than the children of light" (Luke 16:8).

CHAPTER FIFTEEN

Four Examples of
Faith Extenders That Worked

Faith Fed Them

The great prayer warrior, George Mueller, was the director of a faith orphanage in England many years ago. A book I read about his life contained the account of a simple faith extender he used most effectively. It was almost the same faith extender that Jesus used before He fed the 5,000.

One day Mueller found the kitchen cupboard bare. Undaunted by this, he assembled his little orphan band at the dinner table. He ordered the table to be completely set with plates, glasses, napkins and silverware, as if ready for a great feast. There was only one small detail missing; there was not one bite of food on the table. Just imagine the little faith-filled orphans as they looked at the empty milk glasses, pitchers and plates. No matter how much faith you have in God's ability to provide, an empty cupboard speaks loud and clear. Why, as the day went on, even these little orphans, who lived daily by faith, were no doubt shaken.

As Mueller brought the children to attention, he spoke to them with great confidence. "Let us pray and thank God for the good meal He will provide for us today."

In unison, the little band of orphans prayed, "Thank You, Father, for Your concern for us. Thank You for Your promise of continuous, abundant supply. Thank You for this fine meal we are about to eat. Please bless it to our bodies, in Jesus' name. Amen.''

At that very moment, outside the orphanage, a loud crash was heard. The hungry little orphans leaped from their seats at the table and rushed to the windows to see what had happened. The sight that met them was truly astonishing to their little minds. A fully loaded milk, cheese and butter wagon had collided with a bread wagon right at the orphanage's front door. Now, mind you, this is a true story. What do you think was done with all of that milk, cheese and bread? You guessed it! Every loaf of bread, bottle of milk and piece of cheese not ruined in the crash was brought into the orphanage. In the place that the devil had planned for hunger pains to dominate, strong faith brought about a great banquet and full stomachs.

Notice how powerful a faith extender the set table became. Mueller did not stand before the empty cupboard, emphasizing the fact that it was empty. Instead of this, he and his little charges did everything to amplify their faith, positioning themselves for dinner at the fully set table. This simple faith extender kept anticipation alive long enough for supply to arrive.

How will it build your faith to stand in front of your empty cupboard and stare at the empty shelves, allowing them to fill your mind with the hopeless state of things? It will not help you to listen to your own voice speaking the hopelessness of your situation. How can you, with these negative visions and negative words, declare, ''Well, God, we are out of goods, but we are trusting You for sufficiency.'' Any attempted confession made from this position of weakness will only be hollow sounds with no great faith behind them.

If you ever face this most serious dilemma, close the pantry door! Then see yourself sitting down at the table—

not an empty table, but a table that is set. Surely this would bring about stronger faith than would be produced by emphasizing the lack. Some people will think this is foolish and they will never try it. Many who scoff will never experience the miracle of abundance that Mueller and his faith-filled orphans experienced. When bedtime came at the orphanage that evening, the children went to bed with tummies full of hot, buttered bread, delicious cheese and milk. I am sure more than one little orphan thanked God that night that George Mueller was a man who not only knew how to trust God to the fullest, but also knew how to extend their faith to its fullest capacity.

Can't you see how much greater your ability to receive becomes, when you have a positive mental picture of your needs being met by confessing God's promises of bounty and supply? Can you see how much more easily your faith can rise to fill your empty cupboard, as well as supply your other needs, when your words and thoughts are in line with God's promises? A good faith extender can increase your faith's power. Deemphasizing the problem and reinforcing the solution is a sure way to strong faith.

A New Well

Let me illustrate further the power of extending your faith by a good, positive confession. Some time ago, while living in Southern California, I had a new well dug on my property. I was told by reliable sources that I would have to dig to a depth of 280 feet or more to produce a clear, strong stream of water. No well in our immediate area had produced sufficient water for irrigation at less than this depth. There was no guarantee as to the depth we would have to drill to find adequate quantities of water. Once I told the well contractor to begin digging, I was committed. I would be required to invest more money for each foot deeper that he drilled. This would have to continue until good water had been reached. The well was imperative to our landscaping plans. However, I knew it would seriously hinder my landscape budget if I had to drill further than 100 feet.

The success of the whole venture depended on that well coming in at 100 feet, so I employed several faith extenders. I spoke the victory out loud. I said to everyone, "We will hit abundant water at 100 feet!" I also pictured a great pool of water just 100 feet below my house. I saw a lake of water 100 feet down. I did not allow my imagination to see anything else. I prayed fervently to God for the well to come in at 100 feet. Notice this verse:

> Thou shalt also decree a thing, and it shall be established unto thee (Job 22:28).

I decreed that the well would bring forth good water abundantly at 100 feet and that it would require only eighty feet of casing. The well itself was expensive; the casing was twice as expensive. I repeated Job 22:28 night and day. I decreed water at 100 feet. I also believed, with all my heart, that things that I needed to come to pass, in relation to my well, would come to pass. Notice another verse that encourages this type of behavior.

> For verily I say unto you, That whosoever shall say unto this mountain, Be thou removed, and be thou cast into the sea; and shall not doubt in his heart, but shall believe that those things which he saith shall come to pass; he shall have whatsoever he saith. Therefore I say unto you, What things soever ye desire, when ye pray, believe that ye receive them, and ye shall have them (Mark 11:23,24).

I confessed to everyone that my well would come in at no deeper than 100 feet and that there would be no need for more than eighty feet of casing. As you can imagine, I was laughed at by each professional well driller who had bid on the work. When I selected a contractor, I had to ask him not to speak of the absurdity of my statement. I asked him just to say nothing to me about his doubts until after at least 100 feet of drilling had been done. To the amazement of the "professionals," the well came in at 100 feet and, amazingly, required only five feet of casing. This was seventy-five feet less casing than I had budgeted. Within just five feet of the surface, we hit the type of stone that made it unnecessary to have casing for the well.

This well is still producing clear, cool water at over fifty-five gallons per minute, in an area of San Diego county where the best wells produce only fifteen to twenty gallons of water. I could have confessed what every other well owner in that area had confessed—that the water was at 280 feet—and I would have had a 280-foot well just like everyone else. How I thanked God that I had learned how to use good faith extenders like the positive confession and verbalization of the yet unmanifested.

The Old Faithful Washing Machine

Let me share a memorable experience a member of the church I pastored in San Diego had with decreeing by faith and the use of a unique faith extender.

It seems as if the old, faithful family washing machine had broken down. It happened at a time when the expense of having it replaced would have caused the man to miss paying a previously made missionary pledge. With great diligence and resolve, he attempted to fix the ailing appliance. After he had labored over the machine for three hours, it became clear that it was beyond repair. The motor was completely burned out.

After thinking up possible solutions, his wife said, "Honey, you've tried everything else. Why don't we lay hands on it and pray over it? I am sure God can fix it."

There was something in his wife's voice, in her simple declaration that God could, without doubt, fix it. Her positive declaration turned what was fast becoming a state of hopelessness to one of hope. The man's faith was revived by her positive statement. Just imagine the damage that negative words from her would have done to his faltering faith.

For three hours he had labored to fix the washing machine, only to have every attempt fail. His faith was terribly weakened. His expectation of the machine ever again running had now grown very thin, as he had tried again and again to repair it, without result. He said he had tried everything he knew to do, and some things he didn't know to do. He was more than ready to quit, when he heard his wife's faith-filled positive words: "I am sure that God can fix it." His faltering faith drank up those positive words, as a parched man in the desert would drink up fresh cool water. His faith exploded into full force. He quickly agreed with the words of his wife, "Yes, God can fix it."

> Again I say unto you, That if two of you shall agree
> on earth as touching any thing that they shall ask,
> it shall be done for them of my Father which is in
> heaven (Matt. 18:19).

His next words were, "Let's do what Brother John instructed us to do in his sermon last Sunday! Let's, in faith, lay hands on it and speak in agreement that it will work."

So, with strong faith, they prayed over that old, broken-down washing machine, using the Scriptures they had learned the previous Sunday. They declared they would have whatsoever they said, and that when two Christians would agree as touching anything on earth, it would be done. They based their authority behind every demand in the powerful name of Jesus. They described, in loud voices, all of the expected functions the washer should be able to accomplish.

When they had finished praying and decreeing, my friend said that he could see his wife's face fill with doubt. Why, in just the brief moment between praying and reaching out to touch the on switch, doubt had overtaken his wife and her faith was growing weaker by the moment. Without hesitation, my friend said to his doubting wife, "What we need is a good, strong faith extender. Get the dirty clothes and put them into the washer with the soap."

At that point, his wife cautioned him that he ought to test the machine first, because it wouldn't be good to have the liquid soap all over the clothes without immediately having water come into the machine. He exclaimed, "That machine is fixed, in the name of Jesus, and it will work. I have no doubt of it. I see it busily washing clothes."

Separating the colored clothes from the white, they put the clothes into the washing machine. They measured the prescribed amount of detergent. With this action, his wife's faith began to rise again. She said, "I am convinced that when you push that start button, it is going to start."

He said, "Honey, do you believe that with all your spirit, soul and body?"

"I do now," she said. "That faith extender of putting those dirty clothes in the machine, soap and all, has expanded my faltering faith a hundredfold."

They both knew the machine was about to start. "Now, before either one of us can fall into unbelief," the wife said, "let's both put our fingers on the start button and, in unison, rebuke the devil and command the machine to start as we push the start button." With this, they pushed the button and, you guessed it, the machine started to sputter and smoke.

With this my friend slammed his fist down on top of the machine and said, "In the name of Jesus, I said run. I did not say sputter and smoke. Now get in line with what I have commanded." Immediately the machine gave a giant shudder and settled down and operated like a new machine.

This simple faith extender saved my friend and his wife the cost of a new washer and it allowed them to complete their missionary commitment. At my last knowledge of this machine, it was still washing clothes just fine.

Crisco—a Little Dab'll Do Ya

I recall the time when my wife and I had very little in the way of material goods. During this time, we were always desperately short of money. The acuteness of this shortage was obvious.

One morning I was to attend a preacher's conference. As I was getting dressed, I prepared to comb my hair, when I discovered, to my disappointment, that I was completely out of hair oil—not even a drop remained. In desperation, I ended up improvising and using Crisco! Things were very desperate in our finances. The meeting was of tremendous importance to me. I needed desperately to secure a preaching assignment, not only to fulfill my calling, but even more pressing was the need to receive funds to buy needed items, the least of which was hair oil.

Our funds were non-existent. By every outward sign, I was a failure as an evangelist. To break the hold that these depressing circumstances had on me, I employed a faith extender. I pictured myself not as my circumstances said I was, poor and totally destitute. Instead, I pictured myself as God saw me—an anointed evangelist who would easily secure an appointment for a series of meetings. I chose to focus on the reality of what God said I was. I extended my faith by casting down the mental image of my need. I cast down evil imaginations and every high thing (obstacle) that exalted itself against the knowledge of God (2 Cor. 10:5). I chose to focus my thoughts on what God said and not on what my empty pockets were saying.

With Crisco in my hair and with empty pockets, I went to the meeting. And sure enough, I was asked to conduct a great, two-week crusade in Indiana. This key meeting developed into a dozen or more additional appointments.

If I had focused on my inability and lack, I would no doubt have missed the meeting and the invitation to speak in Indiana and perhaps would not be in the ministry today.

I recall another time, however, that the wrong mental picture of myself brought me to a dismal financial circumstance. I found myself hundreds of miles from home, once again broke and dejected, staring at the faded wallpaper in a cheap motel room. I had just finished preaching my heart out in a revival meeting in New Orleans. I was making this rest stop, not because I had extra money for hotel expenses, but out of necessity. I needed to prepare my tired body for the long drive back to my home in Missouri.

The revival meeting had been a mixture of blessings and disappointment. On the one hand, I was elated about the many souls that were saved. On the other hand, I was dejected about the advantage that the pastor had taken of me. I had just opened my love offering envelope and found that my full week of preaching ministry had only brought seven dollars and fifty cents.

What soul damage and heartache the takers of this world cause. I had to trade one of my dress suits and my automobile's only spare tire for enough gasoline to get home. I recall sitting in that sad little motel room, feeling lower than a snake's belly. I was accusing myself and God. With one breath I was saying, "Oh, God, why are You doing this to me?," and with the next breath accusing myself by saying, "You, of all people, are surely not an evangelist. Why don't you go back where you came from, give up preaching and become a bricklayer again?" I was rapidly losing altitude.

Thank God, He still speaks to His children and, even beyond that, thank God He spoke to me that night. His words are still vivid to me: "John, are you an evangelist?"

I said, "No, Lord, I am not. Look at me, I'm so beat down and scruffy-looking. Look at this room. The garage I had before I entered the ministry was nicer than this." Then I stopped in mid-sentence and repented, "Forgive me, Lord; let me start over. Please re-ask the question."

"All right. John, are you an evangelist?"

"Yes, Sir, I am an evangelist. You made me an evangelist. I refuse to see myself as anything other than what You say I am."

I saw myself (in my imagination) speaking to thousands, powerfully preaching under the anointing that He had placed on my life.

The next day I drove home with renewed zeal, describing myself out loud as one of the nation's great evangelists. Within hours of my arrival at home, I received a phone call from Art Wilson, who was, at that time, one of the greatest pastors in America. Without hesitation he invited me to hold a campaign in his church, one of the largest churches in Kansas. This resulted in a highly successful campaign and an offering that eclipsed the largest offering that church had ever given to any visiting evangelist— more than enough! Confessing what was yet unmanifested extended my faltering faith beyond the realm of discouragement and insufficiency into the reality of God's abundant supply.

Today my ministry is a hundredfold larger ministry than

the wildest statement I had made about it on my way home that night. All I did was speak and believe that which God said about me. With these words of faith, I rejected my circumstances and broke their hold on me.

Some might say Art Wilson would have called me anyway. That's what the world would say. But I choose to believe that I will have whatsoever I say. I choose to believe that as I think I am, so I will be. I choose to believe that I can say a thing and it shall come to pass.

Thou shalt also decree a thing, and it shall be established unto thee (Job 22:28).

If the mental picture of failure and the confession of insufficiency is bringing you good success, just continue with it and pay no attention to what I am saying. But, if it is bringing you that which it always brought me, maybe it is time to change your confession and speak only those things God says about you. Maybe it's time to enlighten your imagination with scenes of your success.

CHAPTER SIXTEEN

Summary

True Bible Prosperity Is a Matter of Faith

If you find yourself living in poverty or insufficiency and ever plan to be released from insufficiency's cruel grip, you must begin to see yourself out of insufficiency and in the realm of abundant prosperity.

However, before you can properly visualize that new, prosperous image of yourself, you must be convinced that God has promised to meet every need you might have. Please realize that the conviction of God's ability to supply your every need will not come to you from my teaching or the teaching of others. My teaching might stimulate your mind with the possibilities of God's Word. The teachings of other Bible scholars might motivate you to consider God's solutions to your problems. However, you will have to experience this truth from God's Word on your own.

Let the Word of God speak to you. Hear again the inventory of what God has for you. Allow yourself to hear the next four Bible verses with spiritual ears.

The first verse tells us that all our blessings are spiritual (invisible). The second verse tells us what manner of blessings are provided. It reveals the inventory of the invisible blessings in the heavenly storehouses of God—all things that pertain unto life and godliness (these two realms are all-inclusive). The third verse tells us that God is ready to do more than we can ask or think. The fourth verse tells us that God will give us sufficiency in everything we need.

Blessed be the God and Father of our Lord Jesus Christ, who hath blessed us with all spiritual blessings [invisible] in heavenly places in Christ (Eph. 1:3).

According as his divine power hath given unto us all things that pertain unto life [natural] and godliness [spiritual], through the knowledge of him that hath called us to glory and virtue (2 Pet. 1:3).

Now unto him that is able to do exceeding abundantly above all that we ask or think, according to the power that worketh in us (Eph. 3:20).

And God is able to make all grace abound toward you; that ye, always having all sufficiency in all things, may abound to every good work (2 Cor. 9:8).

The words you have just read are directly from God's Word. They have great power to build your faith. For "faith cometh by hearing, and hearing by the word of God" (Rom. 10:17). Christian books can motivate you. They can challenge you. But they cannot give you faith. Once you *know* God's truth, you will easily change your confession about your adverse circumstances. You will no longer have to say wistfully, "Maybe one day I will have my needs met." Rather you will say boldly, "I am prosperous right now! I have all, and I abound."

When your confession changes by conviction (because you believe what God's Word says), it won't be long until your circumstances will also change. For it is a Bible fact that you shall have whatever you say!

Four Laws

I have found four laws of control over the natural realm to be true. With these you can do much to control your circumstances:

1. You are becoming what you *imagine* yourself to be.
2. That which you continuously *concentrate* on tends to grow stronger, and that which you *ignore* tends to grow weaker.
3. What you daydream about tends to become *reality*.
4. You are being drawn to whatever you concentrate on, and *whatever you concentrate on is being drawn to you*.

While the following scriptures do not use the same words, they do substantiate the four rules that I have shared with you.

For as he thinketh in his heart, so is he (Prov. 23:7).

For the thing which I greatly feared is come upon me, and that which I was afraid of is come unto me (Job 3:25).

Finally, brethren, whatsoever things are true, whatsoever things are just, whatsoever things are pure, whatsoever things are lovely, whatsoever things are of good report; if there be any virtue, and if there be any praise, think on these things (Phil. 4:8).

And if we know that he hears us...we know that we have the petitions that we desired of him (1 John 5:15).

CHAPTER SEVENTEEN

Closing

As faith extender after faith extender comes to mind, 100 more pages could easily be written. I believe the list is endless. For years men and women have devised things that would help them focus on what only strong faith could supply.

Let me say it plainly: I don't know where to stop writing.

Men whom I respect most, in separate circumstances, use different faith extenders.

Let me begin with a faith extender I saw Paul Crouch of the Trinity Broadcasting Network use in a telethon. On missions night of a telethon, we all gathered around the giant globe which was in the middle of the stage. Then his wife, Jan, took a small red dot and stuck it on the globe on a city where she wanted Christian television.

Paul told the television audience, "If you have a favorite city where you would like to see Christian television, call in your pledge and name the city or country, and we will put a red dot on that city." Immediately the phones lit up from across America. Hundreds of calls flooded in with substantial donations. There were so many calls that the whole globe was filled with the little stick-on dots. How quickly strong faith can be ignited! Notice: The need was always there. The globe was there telethon after telethon. But the little red dots were the thing that exploded faith.

Recently I attended a meeting in Denver, Colorado, in which Morris Cerullo was speaking about faith to heal, deliver and supply. He asked for a blank check from the audience. When a man gave him one, Cerullo took the check and signed it with the name: Jesus Christ. Then he held the check up and said, "You fill in the blank for whatever your need is: healing from cancer, salvation of a loved one, finances, restoration of a marriage, whatever you need."

Faith rose to the highest possible level. Without hesitation, people began to praise God and receive from Him all they needed.

How easily a simple blank check, with the name of Jesus written on it, took that which seemed distant and impossible and made it close and attainable.

Start today. Use faith extenders, and see the simplest faith extender help even the weakest faith.

To contact John Avanzini, write:

John Avanzini
P. O. Box 1057
Hurst, Texas 76053

*Please include your prayer requests and
comments when you write.*

Other Books by John Avanzini

Always Abounding

30-60-Hundredfold

Powerful Principles of Increase

Rapid Debt-Reduction Strategies

Stolen Property Returned

War On Debt

The Wealth of the World

**Available from
your local bookstore,
or from**

HIS Publishing Company
P. O. Box 1096
Hurst, TX 76053